A BREAK IN THE SILENCE

RECONCILED OR FORGOTTEN?

DONALD T. HARDISON II

ELIZABETH'S WRITING CORNER

All Bible verses and Scripture references are quoted from the King James Version. "All Scripture is given by inspiration of God, and is profitable for doctrine, for reproof, for correction, for instruction in righteousness: That the man of God may be perfect, thoroughly furnished unto all good works" (2 Timothy 3:16-17).

ISBN: 979-8-9895619-6-4 (eBook)
ISBN: 979-8-9895619-7-1 (Paperback)
ISBN: 979-8-9895619-8-8 (Hardcover)

Library of Congress Control Number: 2025906178

Elizabeth's Writing Corner
Myrtle Beach, SC
https://elizabethswritingcorner.com/

To my son, Donald Michael Hardison III, thank you for having the courage and allowing me to share our story.

This book is also dedicated to all those who have come from broken families and have lived life without the ones they love—fathers, mothers, sons, daughters, and more.

TABLE OF CONTENTS

Introduction

My Strong Desire

Throughout the journey of my life, I have carried a desire for families—fathers, mothers, sons, and daughters. I've especially wanted to see those who are separated and isolated from each other coming back together in reconciliation. I've listened to too many painful stories and seen too many tears to ignore the epidemic of broken families that is sweeping the globe, one that is not only hurting individual people but also causes so much devastation to our world.

If I think back, my desire for families actually began when I was very young and became stronger each year I grew older. As a child, I was given the opportunity to be born in a loving and supportive home with both of my parents, Dad on one side and Mom on the other. Because of their loving example, I became the man I am today with the passion I have for others.

My father was a hard-working man, devoted to providing a life for his family. He was focused on much more than just fulfilling our financial needs. He loved his time with my mother and with all of his children. Meanwhile, my mother was a stay-at-home mom and quite the homemaker. Together, they worked as a team to raise four children, two boys and two girls.

My parents loved and adored us. Their lives were spent raising us, teaching us, and correcting us. They taught us morals and values like respect, honor, and integrity. They showed us the difference between good and evil as they prepared us to grow into adults, individuals who would one day have to go out into the world and become men and women of our own.

Dad and Mom also taught us to always stand up for what was right, especially for those who couldn't stand up for themselves. They showed us by both their words and their actions that our job was not only to care for ourselves but also to always look out for others.

Yet, the most powerful thing my parents taught us was that the greatest gifts in life didn't come with a cost. Above all else, love is the greatest gift that we can give to one another. Love seeks to protect and nurture. Love covers a multitude of sins. Love is the bonding glue that holds us all together.

As I grew from a young boy into a teen and was able to understand these lessons on a deeper level, I also saw firsthand the struggles that my parents faced—not only in their own lives but also in the lives of many others who came in and out of our home. I watched and listened as challenging situations arose and were dealt with one by one. I saw my father overcome his addiction to Valium and alcohol. I saw my mother overcome her fears of her abusive father.

In seeing my parents overcome their own trials, I recognized that life was altogether different for them in the generation that they grew up in. Both my parents had abuse taking place in their homes as children. Times were tough, the Vietnam War was taking place, and good jobs were hard to come by. They also didn't grow up in nice big homes like they provided for me when I was growing up. Families in those days were often larger, which meant less personal time with Dad or Mom and the necessity to share bedrooms with multiple siblings.

When pondering the stories I heard from my parents about their own upbringings, I often thought about how they became the parents I came to know, adore, and love. Together, they truly created a safe refuge and a place of love for me, for which I am forever grateful.

In those days of my childhood, I remember hoping and imagining that I would one day have a family of my own. I envisioned that my own family life would mirror that of my parents when they were raising me. After all, I had a strong foundation with loving parents, a safe home, and all the fundamentals needed to provide the same for my own children one day.

When I became an adult, however, life didn't turn out for me or my children anything like I expected. In fact, it was the complete opposite.

My purpose in sharing my story is not to cast a negative light on the difficulties I have faced. Rather, I desire to bring hope and encouragement to those of you who have also dealt with the hardship of family struggles, especially for parents who have become estranged from one or more of their children and for children who have become alienated from one or both of their parents.

This book tells my own story from two sides of the spectrum: my expectations about what a healthy family should look like and the reality I faced in experiencing how American society seeks to tear families apart. I also walk you through the lessons that I have learned firsthand about living a life outside of what society deems responsible.

If there is one thing I know, it's this: being a family isn't easy and comes with many hardships. Separation can come at any time. Overcoming any family issue takes a lot of work that starts with love and then continues with much understanding, patience, forgiveness, and endurance.

This whole process can be seen as a journey where we take the first major step by deciding to work on ourselves and correct our own shortcomings. From there, we stop the cycle of hurt and pain that has affected past generations, finding complete healing from the many issues we've faced in the past and refusing to pass them on to our own children.

I truly believe that we all have what it takes to build relationships in our lives, from our husbands and wives to the close friends and co-workers we see in our day-to-day lives. While the ability to form deep relationships lies within all of us, whether or not we act on that potential is completely up to us.

Allow me to ask you a few questions that will serve as food for thought as you join me on my journey throughout the rest of the pages of this book:

Have you spent your time building the relationships you desire to have with your family, including your husband or wife, your sons, your daughters, and even your grandchildren?

Have you desired to build relationships with others you love, but the circumstances of life just so happen to get in your way and time seems to be slipping away?

Let me be blunt: even though certain things like work, money, and pursuing a comfortable life take up so much of our time, they don't matter at all in the long run. It's the things that money cannot buy—the greatest things that don't come with a cost—that truly bring us peace and resolution. We all desire to live a life full of purpose and meaning, which starts with happiness in our own homes.

We always prioritize the things that are most important to us, so take some time to consider what's most valuable to you. Please know that it's never too late to start fresh and try again. Your family is counting on you!

This is my story.

CHAPTER ONE

LIFE IS FULL OF UNCERTAINTY

I t had been over a decade since I last communicated with my children, over ten years since I last saw their faces and spoke with each of them. All lines of communication had been completely lost. Their teenage years had vanished before my very eyes. Their high school graduations were over with, and they were now grown adults.

I thought of my children often, and I had so many questions. My questions sounded something like this: Had they gone on to college? Had they gotten married? Had they moved out of their mothers' houses? Were they now navigating life on their own? I had no idea! I desperately desired to know. I needed to know!

Taking a step back from the swirl of my thoughts, being the absent father in my children's lives was definitely not part of my dreams and aspirations for either them or me. I knew how important it was to have both my parents in my life when I was growing up, so naturally, I desired the same exact thing for each of them.

In fact, having lost both of my parents at a young age—my mother when I was twenty-one and my father when I was twenty-five, I knew what life looked like as an orphan and how painful it felt. To say the very least, life was hard as a young man with my parents not being a part of my ongoing story. I didn't have them when I needed to go to them for advice, and of course, I missed their presence on a day-to-day basis.

So, I couldn't imagine what my children were forced to go through, not having me in their lives as teenagers and quickly becoming adults on their own. Most importantly, I wondered if they were hurt, mad, and disappointed with me. Just these thoughts alone crushed me and often brought tears to my eyes. One thing was for sure: I wanted to be there for each of them. I thought about my children all the time, and it broke my heart that I was absent from their lives.

When I was growing up, some of my friends at school had parents who were divorced and others even had fathers and mothers who were in prison. I saw the effect that both scenarios had on my friends and sympathized with the deep loss that they dealt with each and every day. My dad actually became like a father to each of those kids. He was their role model, someone they looked up to and would call upon in times of need. That was the kind of father that I aspired to be like.

Now, looking at my current situation, the worst part of dealing with the internal record that played over and over in my mind was asking myself, "How in the world could this have happened to me and my children?" and "Why did it have to happen this way?" My thoughts raced and my heart broke, knowing that I had somehow brought hurt and pain to my children. They hadn't asked for this grief any more than they deserved it!

As a father and as a man, I felt like I had screwed up! I wasn't even close to being a role model or hero in their lives like my father was to me and all the kids in our neighborhood. I couldn't even be the father that I desired to be for my very own children!

Instead, my children were left to feel the painful weight of loss and speak about their missing dad in the same way that my friends did back in my school days—all the things that broke my young heart when I heard about them happening for the first time.

I had no idea if I would ever be able to make things right, or if I would ever have that chance. All I knew was that I missed each of my children dearly. There was a huge void in my life and my heart without all of them in it.

As I thought about the possibility of making things right, I knew one thing for sure: I am not one to make excuses or to try and justify my choices, or lack thereof. Right is right, and wrong is wrong. Even if it was not my fault in the first place, I still had to take full accountability for the years I had lost out on in my absence.

When it came down to it, I had to make amends. I had to tell them how sorry I was and hope that they would forgive me and allow me to be a part of their lives. I had a deep desire to explain my side of this heartbreaking story, as I knew they were only getting one side of it. I wasn't at all proud to mention many of the details, but nonetheless, I knew this was a topic I had to speak about in an attempt to let my side of the story be heard. I also had to tell the truth in such a way that did not cast blame on any others who were involved.

The more I pondered all the things that I longed to share with my children, my mental list continued to grow. I wanted them to know about the lives of their grandparents. I wanted them to know their family history, their legacy, and their heritage. Of course, I wanted them to hear everything directly from me.

I also wanted my children to know that life wasn't at all easy and that we were not promised tomorrow. I wanted to share my trials and tribulations, my weaknesses, and my strengths with them. I had a strong desire to prepare them for the days ahead. I had a duty to fulfill and a life of experience with which to enlighten them. Yet, the most important thing I wanted to do was to let them know how much I love them and what my life was like without them in it.

Despite all of the hopeful thoughts I had about sharing my story with my children, I couldn't help but think that it was too late. I felt that my window of opportunity had passed. So, I began to ask myself what my parents would do if they were in my situation and how they would fix everything. I knew that if they were still here, they would also be filled with sorrow and stop at nothing to help me keep the family together!

Even though my parents were no longer with me, I knew that with age comes wisdom and understanding, two things I had learned over the years and had to figure out on my own. Better yet, I knew that the Lord would be my guide in this situation since, with Him, all things are possible.

The first thing that came to mind was to dedicate myself to prayer, placing my children in the hands of God Almighty. I had faith that He would watch over them, keep them, and protect them all the days of their lives. After all, that's exactly what my mother did for me. I knew the outcome of that one prayer and what it accomplished in working out the power of transforming my life.

At the same time, praying for my children didn't negate my responsibility to each of them as a father who has always loved and cherished them. My prayers also didn't replace the time I had lost out on with them over the years. In that sense, my prayers were not only my heartfelt request for God to care for my children but also a petition for guidance that He would lead me and give me strength to understand the circumstances that kept me from being the father I always desired to be.

If there is one thing I've learned in my forty-eight years of life, it's this: life is full of uncertainty. The journey set before us is an unforeseen path, full of adventure and misadventure. Life doesn't at all work out in the ways we plan it. The very best we can do is to accept the challenges and obstacles set before us and put our best foot forward each and every day, stopping at nothing to obtain a life worthy of our calling. We do this, not only for ourselves but also for our family, for our friends, and especially for our children.

I recognized the uncertainty in my own life, especially when I thought about how much time I had lost out on with my children. One of the worst realizations that haunted me was that I had not created any memories with them as their father during their high school years.

Once again, I realized that life wasn't anything like I had planned for myself as a child. In fact, life does not share the events that will happen in our futures ahead of time. Instead, we watch everything unfold as it will, day by day, waiting to see what will take place.

Life brings forth many unexpected hardships, trials, and tribulations. Most of the time, we do not even know how to handle these situations at first, having never gone through them before. We need to learn each new lesson one step at a time.

Out of all of the different events of life, having children and becoming a parent is supposed to be one of the most exciting times in a person's life. Yet, it's not always like that. Thinking back to my friends at school and seeing what happens to many families, I began to ask various questions: What happens when you as a new dad or a new mom are unexpectedly incarcerated and unable to see your child for years on end? Or, what happens when you are forcibly driven out of your children's lives by an ex-spouse? What can you do to keep the peace for the sake of your children, even when that ex-spouse is hellbent on breaking the bond between you and your child, maliciously seeking to eliminate you from your rightful position as a parent? Or, how do you handle being left in an orphanage, never knowing your parents or where you came from?

While all these situations may seem like extreme cases for parents and children to face, the truth is that they happen more frequently than many people realize. It's just not commonly spoken about among the mainstream because of the very deep hurt and pain that takes place in the hearts and lives of every person involved.

The reality is that all of these painful situations have serious ramifications for both the parents and the children. Divorce, separation, alienation, estrangement, and abandonment are not simply terms used to apply to social issues but are symptoms of a pandemic that has hurt and broken the hearts of loving parents and children all around the world. Although the reasons for how and why parents and children become estranged from one another vary in severity from simple disagreements to separation due to death, every situation carries feelings of disconnection and unwanted-ness that weigh heavily upon the hearts of all affected.

I knew that something had to be done to stop this type of hurt and pain for both parents and children around the world. I was determined to try and prevent this from happening further to others. Deep within my heart, I was convinced that the story of one man's life told in his own voice would be a message of courage. I also know that such a testimony held the power to inspire others and transform their lives. But who would tell this story?

I had already become that man who sought to make a change everywhere I went, using my personal story to touch the hearts and lives of so many people that I regularly encountered. Of course, while I wanted to make a big difference in the world we all live in, I cared much more about helping my own children as they grew older.

As I came to understand all of these things, I was determined to build my own foundation for my children and grandchildren. It was something that I could one day pass down to them, proving the lasting impact of my legacy and the very great love that I had harbored for them since the very beginning. With that, although the path ahead remained uncertain, I hung onto hope and a prayer and kept moving forward.

CHAPTER TWO

HEARTBREAK IN THE MISSION FIELD

As I continued my work in the mission field, I came across a lot of struggling people, both on the streets and in their own homes. Many came from broken families, and they were all willing to share their stories with me. While each person had a different experience about how they were raised and what troubles they had endured, I noticed there were several distinct patterns taking place in all of their situations.

I first spoke with men and women who were fathers and mothers and had become alienated from their children. Their stories were heartbreaking to hear, even as they sounded a lot like my own.

These people spoke of the loss they felt and how they were dealing with it internally. They spoke of divorce and how one parent pitted the children against the other parent. They spoke of the arguments their children heard between the two spouses and how the children endured it. It was never the parents' intention for the children to have to face such a negative impact, yet the damage had already been done.

These fathers and mothers saw themselves as the so-called losing parent and talked about how they figured it was best to remove themselves from the situation altogether. They wanted to stop the pain they saw their children going through, so they assumed that it was in the best interest of their children for them to no longer be in the picture.

At the end of the day, this was an extremely tough decision for that parent to make. Often, their children became deeply hurt by the parent's choice to remove themselves from the situation. Yet, being too young to understand the hurt and loss that the absent parent was also going through, those young people thought they were unwanted and abandoned. As a result, the children were filled with resentment and no longer wanted anything to do with their parent.

Some of the parents spoke about how they fought for their children, trying to stay in their children's lives despite the additional pain they knew it would cause. They talked about how the court system was a mess and how they endured many legal battles while fighting for shared parenting to no avail.

For those who may not be aware, the courts in many states in America normally award full custody to the mother in divorce and separation cases. Most commonly, a guardian ad litem is assigned to represent the best interests of any minor children, and the case is then decided according to the guardian's recommendations.

This essentially means that the judge's official ruling is determined by the opinions of others who are considered to be experts and friends of the court. All said, it is a terrible process to drag your children through these court cases. It is also horribly painful for the parent who desires to still be part of the broken family.

When looking back and reflecting on everything I've seen and heard about such cases, I often ask, "Who is there to pick up the broken pieces in the aftermath of such a complex and troubling situation?" and "Who is there to help mend families and bring these hurting individuals together again, especially after the children are considered old enough to make their own choices in the matter?"

When putting these questions to the parents I've spoken to over the years, they often felt at a loss. They did not know how to answer those questions. After all, they believed that they did everything they could for their children, and still to no avail.

The stories of pain went on. These parents spoke of how they wished they could still be there to speak into their children's lives. They mentioned the addictions to drugs and alcohol that became a part of their everyday practices, as they tried to numb the heartache and fill the void caused by their child's absence. They admitted that such addictions were a way of escape rather than a solution, which only made matters worse.

I sympathized with these parents. I told them that I deeply understood their pain, as I was also estranged from my own children and knew first-hand what they were going through. They were curious to hear my story, so I shared more details with them. Yet, I truly wanted peace and happiness for them, so I also was careful in what I said, doing everything I could to avoid adding stress and inflicting more emotional duress on them.

After sharing all of these things, I asked the parents if they wanted to pray with me, not only for our children but also for the other parent, otherwise known as the residential parent or the custodial parent. My hope in this act of grace and kindness was to offer up a prayer of love, peace, forgiveness, strength, and reconciliation for all parties involved. I also prayed for wisdom, knowledge, understanding, and patience.

If there was one thing these children needed, it was to know how much their absent parents loved and needed them. I also knew that many of these children wanted to reconnect with their absent parents but just didn't know how to. After all, both the parents and I felt the same emptiness inside that could only be filled again by having our children back in our loving arms to embrace. We could only imagine the type of pain that our children were also experiencing.

Yet, in the midst of my conversations, I couldn't help but feel my own disgrace and shame. I still felt as if I had failed my children on many different levels. However, I also knew that I was going through a process of accountability and learning how to heal from my own pain. It all started by being able to admit my guilt to others and speak of my heavy burden of not knowing how to bring my children back into my life.

The next group of people that I had the opportunity to meet was made up of young men and young women between the ages of fourteen and eighteen. I saw them all for who they really were: children living on the streets. Some were runaways, others felt they had no home to return to, and all of them no longer found their childhood homes to be a safe haven or refuge from the many obstacles they were facing in their young lives.

These children were the ones without the other parent. Whether it was due to divorce, death, separation, or incarceration, these kids were homeless. Even though they felt like they were forced to wander around on the streets, they figured that at least it was a place to get away from what they felt hurt them the most.

It always seemed to me that I would frequently just so happen to cross their paths. Without knowing how the encounter would go, I always gave a nod to say, "Hello," and offered a simple, "How are you doing today?"

To my surprise, they would begin to chat with me. Of course, they were always hungry, looking for a cheeseburger, fries, and a drink. I was glad to get them a bite to eat, just for the chance to be able to sit down with them and hear their stories.

No matter their age or situation, all of them spoke of a feeling of abandonment and how they were left thinking that they were unloved and unwanted by the very people who brought them into the world. They also mentioned how much they missed their absent parent, how the separation had negatively affected them, and how often they wondered if their lives would have turned out a lot differently if both their dad and their mom had remained in their lives.

Our conversations often led to plenty of tears as they spoke of the deep hurt they carried. I couldn't help but extend my arms to them, hoping to hug them and reassure them that although their journey had been hard, prayer and hope for reconciliation one day would be their guide.

To my amazement, these young people would ask me if we could pray together, not for themselves but for the one who had been absent from their lives all along. They truly cared about each of their parents, mentioning how much they missed their father or mother and thought a lot about them.

Their prayers were always positive, wanting their absent parent to be well and in good health, with hopes of never being forgotten. Even if they didn't say it in words, I knew what was really in their hearts: a longing to know that their missing parent would always love and remember them.

After praying together, I encouraged these young people to keep on the pathway of forgiveness, warning them not to allow the circumstances of this world to harden their hearts due to what they had already been dealing with. I assured them that there were always multiple sides to a story and that all sides needed to be heard. They agreed with me, sharing with me their desire to hear the side of their absent parent one day.

At the same time, these children were well aware that hearing the side of their absent parent could change the way they looked and felt towards their residential parent. Either way you look at it, it's a hard weight to place on a child at any age. They are completely innocent in the matter and never asked for this type of burden in the first place, yet it was given to them to deal with.

I also shared my own story with them, speaking of my own loss and my own hopes for my children in the days ahead. In response, they told me to find my children, even if it was only to tell them how much I loved them.

Besides the parents and the children that I met and spoke with, there was a third group: families who appeared to be merely cohabiting, living under the same roof but struggling separately with many different issues. Despite the two parents still living together, they had become estranged and alienated from each other and from their own children.

Most parents had a strong desire to provide a comfortable life for their children instead of forcing the family to deal with any type of struggles, whether because they remembered past hardships they faced when growing up or since they feared putting their children under any new troubles. As a result, work commonly took the grand stage within their homes, and their children were left to go by the wayside.

While the parents' intentions for their children's future were good, they were completely unaware that their children sat right in front of them, craving attention that they desperately needed. After all, when a child does not receive the attention they naturally need from both parents to grow up healthy and whole, resentment creeps in and the children are left to their own devices.

As I recognized this type of neglect taking place within families, I also recognized how society as a whole was changing for the worse. The things that our children were learning in public school deliberately intended to distance family members from each other. Instead of us parents raising our children to feel safe within the walls of our homes, we allowed them to be raised in institutions that planned to separate generations and make parents the enemy.

Our children also did not feel safe within the walls of the schools they attended because of the rising violence in culture as a whole. Many parents sent their kids to school, expecting them to find a safe place to learn and connect with peers. Instead, our children had to be protected by law enforcement due to threats of bombings, mass shootings, and more.

As I thought about it further, I could see how children were facing insecurities, hurt, and pain on their own, which led to other alarming trends. It seemed like every time I turned on the news, I heard about a new crime being committed by a child or a new tragedy targeting innocent children. Teenage suicide was on the rise. Mass shootings were becoming part of our new norm. What was even more alarming was that the gunmen behind these shootings were our very own children!

It was obvious to me that the problem starting in broken families was only made worse by the education system. Our children were regularly in grave danger of being targeted, bullied, and manipulated. Instead of being taught wholesome truths like I had been brought up with, kids were introduced to new ideas that left them without a solid foundation. Confusion filled the atmosphere and common sense, morals, and values were tossed to the wind.

All the while, our children were left without anyone to turn to and had to pretty much figure out life for themselves. The trust they once had for parents, teachers, and other adults had become broken, leaving them to a world all of their own.

Ultimately, resilient children find ways to cope, even if it means raising themselves, so to speak, and becoming prematurely independent. Other children act out to get the attention they both need and desire, which normally results in them being diagnosed and medically treated as if they have some kind of disease.

At times, the parents that I would meet with in their own homes would ask me for counsel. Having seen all kinds of things that were taking place in society, schools, and families, I was ready to share what I had learned. I brought insight from the two other groups that I had already spent time with—the parents who no longer had their children in their lives and the children on the streets who no longer had their parents in their lives.

I explained to these families how important it was for them to develop quality time together, reminding them that we are never promised tomorrow. I talked about how the choices we make today affect us tomorrow, especially since time was something that we could never get back. I hoped to give them a broader perspective beyond their little career bubbles, telling these parents that what they were working so hard for sat right in front of their eyes and were just begging for their attention—their own children!

Of course, I always sought to focus on the positive, encouraging these parents that it was never too late for them to bring their family back together as a whole, starting today and continuing every day for the rest of their lives. I knew in my heart that building and maintaining close relationships were the biggest things a family could hope for. After all, commitment was a major desire that I had focused on throughout my life, so what else could any loving parent truly wish to see for their whole household but close personal and deep emotional relationships between each family member?

The last group I encountered was during my visits to the local orphanages. It was one of the most painful situations for me to see, even as our times together were filled with joy and laughter. I spent a lot of time with children who really and truly had no one there for them—no parents, no family, and no one to love them as they deserved to be loved.

My visits with them were always bursting with fun as we made it a time of creativity, arts and crafts, and games. No matter how enjoyable those days were, the reality of their outcomes often hit me as bleak.

After my visits, I would sit quietly in my car, remembering their smiling faces and the many questions they would ask. Tears would begin to stream from my eyes, knowing from my own experience firsthand what it was like to be without parents. I was certain that it was much harder for them, since they were still just little children.

Having done my research, I knew that a child tends to have a much better life when raised by both their mother and their father in a loving home. The chance of a child being successful was far less when raised in a single-family home, so I could only imagine what the percentage was for orphans. While the numbers, statistically speaking, were staggering, they don't fully address the deep hurt and pain these beautiful souls have to deal with.

Despite my sadness, I knew how important every visit was to them. They always remembered what day and time I would be coming each week and always looked forward to it with great excitement and anticipation. It reminded me how important it is to follow through on your words with real action for all children, but especially for very young kids. All they seek is loving attention, so knowing that someone cares enough to come spend time with them truly means the world to these little ones!

After thinking about my experiences in ministering to these four groups of hurting people, I knew that something had to be done. What else could I do but continue the work I had already started? I often felt like a lonely man faced by a society that, as a whole, had taken a turn for the worse. Something had to change, and I had to prepare myself for whatever came next.

In my personal life, I was bound and determined to somehow reenter my children's lives, even as they were now young adults with lives of their own. After all, I needed them, and they also needed me, even if they were not yet ready to admit it. At the very least, I had to try to reconnect with my children. Despite how hard this would be for both them and me, I would be making an effort, not only for my family but also for the generations to come.

Meanwhile, on the larger scene, I aspired to become a voice and megaphone of hope, an advocate for all of the parents and children whose voices had been silenced and left searching for a solution. I always had a desire to help families, so seeing a whole generation in need of healing within a world lacking love gave me a deeper passion to press on!

CHAPTER THREE

THE JOURNEY OF A PARENT

Throughout my years of growing up and becoming a father of my own, I have learned a lot of things when it comes to parenting. I've especially seen how becoming a parent isn't at all easy and comes with a huge responsibility for both the father and the mother.

For starters, I truly believe that children are the biggest miracles given to us by God. Since they are gifts of love from above, our children need to be treated as such. They look to us for guidance, safety, security, and most importantly, love and affection.

Yet, what happens when that sense of security is taken from our children? As I've mentioned before, the separation between us and our kids can result from divorce, death, incarceration, or other tragic events. Life doesn't share what will unfold in the future.

All of our children need someone to look up to and feel connected to. It's human nature for them to want to feel connected to us, a desire to be a part of something greater than themselves. If our children do not receive those natural needs from us as parents, they will seek and search for others to fill that role in their lives in hopes of replacing what they first lost.

Here's another way to think about it: when our children do not receive the love and attention they require, they feel abandoned. Whether they are physically or emotionally separated from us, they hurt deeply inside and their hearts have been broken by the very ones they love and trust the most. We as parents are the ones who are supposed to protect them and always be there for them in their times of need, but we have actually been the ones to let our own children down in one way or another.

If we as parents truly take accountability for our own actions, we will start by seeing how our choices play a critical role in the emotional well-being of our children. For instance, divorce is never easy and can get very nasty at times, especially when children are involved. Due to the hurt and pain of our broken marriages, we might want to start casting blame on our spouses, which in turn leads to all kinds of negative effects on our kids.

When we as parents try to pit our children against the other parent, thinking we are protecting them from the type of pain that we have already endured, we are actually making matters worse. We need to ask ourselves: "Did we actually love that person at one time?" and "Do we truly want what is best for them right now?" Then the bigger question is this: "Why would we attempt to break the bond, creating what is called parent–child alienation, and only cause added and unneeded pain to an already tough situation?"

Our children need both parents in their lives, especially from the time of birth and throughout their adolescent years. It's a tender time of molding and maturing as we teach them the things that we as adults have already learned through life itself. I've seen and experienced the cause and effect on children who have not been fortunate enough to have both parents in their lives during these formative years.

Speaking from the perspective of an alienated parent, it's a heartbreaking experience to know your child is without you and vice versa. Your heart and mind feel the loss each and every day. The separation and broken bond haunt your every waking moment with a gaping emotional hole in your heart that only your child can fill.

The truth is that any attempt to hurt an ex-spouse, but not our child, actually results in much worse: hurting all parties involved. Even though we might think we are protecting our children from pain, we are actually setting them up for future failure.

As parents, we desire the very best for our children, so we feel a sense of protection to keep them from the things that once hurt us. While there are many different ways to go about shielding our children from harm, we as parents must be very careful with the words we choose to describe the unfortunate events that have happened in the past. This includes the way we talk about all those who may have been involved in difficult periods of our lives.

We desire to talk to our children about what's right and wrong, to keep them from going down a path that will lead to more trouble and heartache in the end. Unfortunately, for some of us, our voice has been silenced and our presence has been withheld from our children, making our ability to teach them about life that much more difficult.

No one ever said life was easy, but what can we do as parents who see how our children have been left to suffer the loss and pain of years gone by? For me, the first step in finding resolution was prayer, through which I searched for understanding, peace, and a solution. Part of that path meant that I had to learn how to let go of the problems that I had no control over and surrender those to God.

To be honest, there were a lot of things that I tried to do in my own strength. Yet, it seemed like no matter how hard I tried to "fix it" and set things straight, the worse everything became. Spending money on lawyers didn't help because the courts were one-sided on matters like this, and show-

ing up unannounced to see my children definitely didn't work because it only resulted in
getting the cops called on me.

I also faced many false allegations, which led
to me being served a protection order and a
promise of jail time if I ever broke that. It never
made any sense to me, as the protection order
is always granted to the mother but not to the
children, unless the child in question is thought
to be in a harmful or dangerous situation. However, a surprise visit to see your child or calling
the mother's phone to reach your son or daugh-
ter is a direct violation of the order, coming with
an automatic arrest and jail time.

Have you ever been in that situation before? I
have, and for what crime? Longing to be a father
to my very own children! On my part, there was
never any harmful intent. I simply wanted to be
a good dad to my kids.

To make a long story short, after having put in much effort on my own part and fighting a long uphill battle, I saw that my actions to try and fix it were doing nothing. In fact, I could see the negative effect it had on both me and my children. At that point, I figured it was best to let go and surrender the whole situation to God. I could only hope that, one day, when my children were old enough, they would want to reach out to me to continue the relationship we once had.

It was an extremely hard choice for me to make, especially when birthdays and holidays came and went. It was impossible for me to spend quality time with the ones I loved most—my children. I truly desired to be with my kids during these times, but I felt it was in my children's best interest that I not try and force the issue.

What made my choice all the more difficult was that I had already lost both of my parents. In many ways, it felt like everything I had ever come to know and love in life had disappeared, vanishing before my very eyes. Plus, I could already foresee how much pain would continue to haunt my children and me. I felt as if my back was against the wall, stuck on a difficult road of legal battles that came with many unwarranted circumstances when I simply desired to spend time with my kids.

Thinking through this, I knew I had to press on in my quest to become a better man each new day than I was the day before. I had a deep desire to rise above every painful situation and not allow any hurt and resentment to get the better of me, which might in turn cause me to react in a way that was unbecoming of a man of integrity.

After all, I was already going through the process of becoming a man of forgiveness, a man of understanding, a man of peace, a man of patience, and a man of honor. In some ways, it still felt like I had a long road to travel, but I had already come so very far. I already knew what it meant to be broken, crushed by grief, and bewildered by a sense of abandonment. Better yet, I knew Who had healed me, held the answers I sought, and continued to refine my character for the days ahead.

Even as I saw how I was growing and maturing, every time I took a step back to look at the times we lived in, I recognized that a great deal had changed since I was a child. Society as a whole had taken a turn for the worse. Morals, values, and common sense had been pushed to the wayside, making way for what was thought of as the new norm. Divorce rates were skyrocketing, making broken families and single parenting the new standard for American households.

As I've already mentioned, a great shift was taking place where most children were now being raised by schools, peers, and media instead of by their parents. I recognized very early on that this meant my children were being taught new ideas under a new philosophy, which did not align at all with my core family values.

The rise of social media only made this widespread problem worse, creating a virtual playground where our children were now glued to their technological devices. While not yet having the maturity level to understand many of the things they encountered online, our children were exposed to violence, sexual content, and much more every single moment. As a result, young kids were at a greater risk of being exploited, kidnapped, and bullied in the very institutions that claimed to care for them.

Meanwhile, the design of social media offered an easy and addictive trap for our children to fall into, right under our very noses. As if losing one parent wasn't bad enough, many of our children became alienated from both parents. The first parent was separated due to the legal battles, and now our kids were also being drawn away and estranged from their residential parent while still living under the very same roof!

Our children found that the only way they could cope with their feelings of loss and abandonment was to bond with their peers who were also dealing with the same issues. We as parents no longer offered help and were portrayed as irrelevant, so our children and their peers found understanding for the hurt and pain on social media, bonding together on the very platforms that separated them from us in the first place.

I recognized that, in many ways, we parents failed our children. Regardless of whether or not it was actually our fault, I knew in my heart that it was time to take accountability and change the downward spiral. We as a society could no longer continue to allow the ones whom we loved the most—our children—to be drawn away from us.

Yet, there was a troubling trend standing in my way. I noticed that while all of these issues affect an extremely large percentage of people and families in one way or another, these subjects are rarely talked about in the mainstream. It felt like most people were happy to collectively sweep these critical issues under the rug, instead of honestly conversing about these problems and challenging them so that we could defeat them once and for all!

While it's been said that ignorance is bliss, all of these societal issues that we have failed to pay attention to have stolen so much valuable time and memories from each one of us. Today's children are tomorrow's future! The point of being a family was never that we parents should allow our children to rely on institutions for personal growth and guidance.

I knew that it was time to ring the warning bell, something that should have been done long ago. Even for any parents who feel that their voices have been silenced due to their own particular situations, there's always a new opportunity to speak and make a difference for both this generation and for generations to come. That time is now!

CHAPTER FOUR

A TRIP DOWN MEMORY LANE

In September of 1995, I first found out that I was going to be a father. I was nineteen years old and feeling scared, nervous, and excited all at the same time.

I remember the day that I decided to break the news to my parents. They already had two grandchildren—boys, to be exact—and this would be the third grandson. Yet, this one was different.

Upon hearing the news, my dad, who was standing next to me with a cup of coffee in his hand, was unable to contain his joy. He looked over at me, set his cup of coffee on the table, and then pulled me in for a hug. He had a huge smile on his face as he gave me his congratulations. It was the news he had been hoping and waiting for!

My mom was also shocked and excited at the same time, and I think the news brought a lot of joy to her as well. My parents just loved knowing that another grandchild was coming into their lives.

My dad, picking his coffee cup back up off the table once again, looked at me and said, "You're going to name him after us, of course!"

Honestly, I hadn't really thought about it.

"Three Donnies? As if two were not enough!" I said aloud as I chuckled, looking back over at my dad. After a moment's reflection, I added, "Donnie the Third—it's perfect!"

A smile came across his face as he said, "I've been waiting long enough and, finally, I will have a little Donnie as my grandson!"

Meanwhile, my mother looked back at us with tears of joy in her eyes. She said, "It's settled then! What's better than having two Donnies to love and care for than having a third!" She smiled again, as the thought of now having three grandsons gave her an even greater purpose. After having lost her mother, it was as if her grandchildren brought new meaning back into her life.

I felt honored that my dad asked me to name my son after us. After all, I looked up to him. He was by far the greatest man I ever knew, and not to mention, he was my hero. I was also happy because I could tell that my parents loved my son before they even met him. They already couldn't wait to hold him and love on him.

On May 2 of the following spring, Donald Michael Hardison III was born, weighing in at six pounds, nine ounces and measuring nineteen and a half inches long. He had jet-black hair and beautiful brown eyes.

From day one, Donnie, Jr., was bigger than life and showed natural charisma. Everyone who encountered him was drawn to him. It wasn't just because he was a beautiful newborn. No, there was something more to his character. He just had a way about him that told us that he was born to do great things. He still maintains the same charm and appeal to this day.

Sadly, my son never really got the opportunity to get to know his grandmother, since she passed away unexpectedly when he was only one and a half years old. I will say, though, that she fell in love with Donnie, Jr., the first time she laid eyes on him and thoroughly enjoyed every moment she had with him.

My father, on the other hand, will forever stay in my son's memory. They had an instant bond, both being smitten with one another. My dad even had a special name for Donnie the Third. He called him his "Little Ricky Ricardo," properly known as Desi Arnaz from the famous TV show, "I Love Lucy." After all, my son did look a lot like the famous actor.

My son became my father's shadow, filling the shoes I once walked in as a child. They were inseparable! My father used to make his own strawberry jam, and Donnie, Jr., loved it. Every time the two of them were together, little Donnie's face was covered in jam. My dad would never let him leave without sending two jars back home with him. They were quite the pair!

My son was only five years old when my father took his own life. Despite being so young, I could tell that my dad's death affected Donnie, Jr., deeply. To this day, my son hasn't touched strawberry jam and wants nothing to do with it.

I remember telling him once when he was a bit older and able to understand, "Just because your grandfather is in heaven and can't be with us right now doesn't mean you have to stop eating the strawberry jam I know you love. I'm positive he wouldn't want you to go without having what you once enjoyed and looked forward to eating!"

But even those words of comfort didn't change my son's mind on the matter.

As Donnie, Jr., grew up, it became evident that he was all heart. He was kind, caring, and compassionate, and he cared more about others than he cared for himself. He also had a protective spirit, only wanting what was best for everyone in his life.

Throughout his school years, my son was extremely athletic, playing all different kinds of sports from a very young age—baseball, wrestling, football, and even running cross-country. Donnie, Jr., was strong, and he was fast. He had legs the size of old Civil War cannons and ran the hundred-meter dash in a mere ten point nine seconds!

My son was truly a hometown hero to his classmates and friends, putting his heart into everything he did. I loved watching him compete against others. Just showing up to his games and various meets always put a smile on my face, as it did his.

I remember the times that Donnie, Jr., and I spent together, whether it was in person at my place or when he was at his mother's house. We loved to watch the *Lord of the Rings* trilogy. Something about that movie series drew his attention and fascination.

My son and I also played PlayStation 3 together, sometimes into the wee hours of the morning as we talked back and forth on our earpieces. It was a great way to connect with each other, and it always gave us something to look forward to.

During his weekend visits, Donnie, Jr., would help me around the house and tinker around with me in the garage. One year, I was working on restoring an old Jeep Wrangler that I had put a 350 small-block engine in, complete with mud tires.

I even surprised my son one winter by going out and purchased two snowmobiles, both Ski-Doos. His was an MXZ 500 and mine was an MXZ 1000. Both were like rockets on skis, lightning-fast and full of power.

Donnie, Jr., was thrilled! He loved to ride with me at night with just the moonlight as our guide. It became one of our favorite pastimes each year as we looked forward to the winter months ahead together.

On one particular weekend, we had a major snowstorm coming our way. The news of it excited Donnie, Jr., to no end. He kept looking out the window as the snow continued to fall in great, thick flakes.

At last, unable to keep silent, he turned to me and said, "You know what this means, right?"

I played coy with him, but I knew exactly what he was driving at. I said to him, "No, not really, but what does it mean?"

He was quick to reply. "You and me. Tonight. It's time to ride!"

I looked back at him, seeing the anticipation gleaming in his eyes, and said with as much nonchalance as I could muster, "Maybe. We'll see."

You see, I had been up all night, working a third shift. Then I had been up all day, spending time with him. I was pretty exhausted!

I could immediately see the disappointment in his eyes. My answer definitely didn't sit well with him.

He urged me again, "But, Dad, it's the first blizzard of the season, and it's perfect for riding! And, by the way, I just so happened to notice that you have them all filled up with gas."

I looked at him, seeing his excitement, and told him, "Well, Son, it seems to me you have this all planned out."

He smiled back at me and gave me his trademark saying, "I doooo!"

I started a fresh pot of coffee, determined to make his dream a reality. I knew that he and I would be setting out shortly to enjoy the frigid temps, racing back and forth at over one hundred miles per hour as we launched our rockets on skis through the air.

The night had come, and we were all suited up in our gear. The snowmobiles were loaded and strapped down on the trailer, and our helmets were in our hands as we both hopped up in my truck.

Donnie, Jr., and I took the quick drive over to the church where we often went to ride. It was the perfect location: a huge open field, decent-sized hills, and all the room we needed to really open these sleds up.

As soon as we arrived, my son and I set out, ripping it up and leaving kicked-up snow clouds behind us. We raced each other across the snow-covered flats and our skis came off the ground in full throttle.

Donnie, Jr., took off in one direction and I went in another. We were having a blast! As I saw my son out in the distance, I decided I would shoot for the hill that would launch me into the night air. As I carried through with my plan, I went flying through the sky, feeling the familiar exhilarating rush of adrenaline.

Suddenly, my fun came to an abrupt halt. As I landed, one of my skis must have hit a rock underneath the snow, twisting the machine and throwing me from my snowmobile. I landed ungracefully on my head and shoulder, and the last thing I heard was a snap and a pop. I had broken my left collarbone and knocked myself completely unconscious!

As I lay there, completely unaware of what just happened to me, my son came cruising by. He saw my sled upside-down and me on my back, motionless.

Donnie, Jr., quickly parked his machine and came over to me. "Dad... Dad? Are you okay?" His voice was calm, cool, and collected. He automatically knew what had happened to me, having been knocked unconscious before when playing football.

Stooping down, my son opened the broken visor of my helmet and called to me again. "Dad?"

This time, I finally started coming to. I heard his voice as if from far away and struggled to respond. "Where am I?" I asked, blinking up at him.

Donnie, Jr., told me, "Dad, you just crashed your sled. Are you okay?"

Still feeling lost, dazed, and confused, I told him that I was okay, but that I could tell that I had broken my collarbone.

My son helped me sit up and then let me take my time getting up on my feet. From there, he guided me to the truck, helping me into the passenger seat before turning on the engine and putting the heater on full blast to keep me warm.

Donnie, Jr., looked at me for a moment to make sure I was okay and then simply said, "I'll be back." He disappeared from sight as he closed the truck door behind him.

As I sat there in silence, being in immense pain and still regaining full consciousness, my son went straight to work. He loaded up both sleds and strapped them tight to the trailer. As soon as he was finished, he knocked on the passenger side window to let me know we were ready to go. I motioned for him to get into the driver's seat, as I knew I was in no condition to drive.

As my son got behind the steering wheel, I asked him, "Have you ever driven before?"

He nervously responded, "Uhm, no, I'm only fourteen."

I looked at him and said, "Well, it looks like you're getting your first lesson today." Seeing the worried look that immediately came across his face, I told him, "You'll be just fine."

From there, I coached Donnie, Jr., through every step to get us back home. I showed him how to make sure the truck was in four-wheel drive before starting out. I told him to take it slow and to make sure to turn wide so we didn't take out any stop signs when turning onto the next street.

Three short blocks later, we safely arrived home. Pulling up in front of the house, he helped me out of the truck and took me inside to get me situated. After that, Donnie, Jr., went right back out into the cold where he unloaded the sleds and put them into the garage. He finished up by dropping the trailer in its spot and parking the truck beside it.

The next morning, I was grabbing a hot cup of coffee when my son took a break from playing on his PlayStation to come upstairs and check on me. He immediately noticed that I was moving ever so slowly due to the pain I was in.

Donnie, Jr., asked me, "How are you feeling this morning?"

I looked at him and told him that I had seen better days.

He chuckled and said, "I bet you have. That was one crazy night!"

I continued to think about my son's actions long after he left at the end of his weekend visitation. The way Donnie, Jr., took charge of a situation that had gone wrong at such a young age made me very proud of him. Not to mention, he saved my life that night by keeping me from shock and hypothermia. To this day, we still talk about that wild snowmobile ride and how he was the hero of the night!

Another memory I had about my son was more difficult to remember. It all started during another weekend visit when we were heading to church together on a Sunday morning.

At the time, this wasn't really something that Donnie, Jr., was into, but he had met the pastor some days before and seemed to like him. He figured that any friend of my dad's was a friend of mine, and rightfully so.

Donnie, Jr., was curious to see what this man was all about behind the pulpit. Little did we know, we were in for a huge shock—one that we were not at all prepared for.

After the service began in its normal way of three songs followed by the collection basket being passed around, Pastor Jamie took the grand stage and began to speak to the congregation.

Before we knew it, he was calling my son up to the front for all to see. Initially, I figured it was a way of Pastor Jamie welcoming Donnie, Jr., to the church, but it turned out to be anything but that.

Jamie began to say that God had spoken to him on the previous night and that it was time to bring correction to one young man who was present. (My son!) As the man began to say some pretty harsh things to Donnie, Jr., I immediately put a stop to it and called my son back to me. I looked at Jamie with eyes that would pierce a man's soul, collected my family, and left.

The congregation could not believe what they had just witnessed! It was especially unfathomable, since Jamie knew very little about Donnie, Jr., in the first place.

Understandably, my son had a lot to say on the matter since it was his first visit. Surprisingly, his words were not harsh, but he merely mentioned that Jamie had issues and had no business being in a position of leadership.

In response, I assured my son that the situation wasn't over yet. I told Donnie, Jr., that as soon as I knew the service was over, Jamie and I were going to have a man-to-man conversation. I already knew that this was going to be one talk that Jamie was not going to enjoy!

Soon, it was time for that conversation to be had. I put Pastor Jamie in his place, calling for an apology to both my son and my whole family! He reluctantly obliged, but it was obvious that he didn't like someone telling him how he should act in his own church. I further warned him, telling him that if he continued to carry on with this behavior that he would lose the church.

Well, after that day, others came forward to speak about having the same things happen to them and their families. Despite those situations, they continued to be a part of a church that had gone wrong.

I knew that what was happening wasn't right and did not line up with the word of God. I also was convinced that Jamie was not hearing from God like he told everyone he was. I began making some phone calls to the higher-ups, calling for an investigation into Jamie's actions.

To make a long story short, two weeks later, Jamie was removed from the office of pastor, and the church doors were shut for good. Yet, despite that conclusive ending, I was concerned about the possible long-term effects it could have on my son, especially at his age. I wondered if it would give him a reason to avoid believing in Jesus or living a life of faith.

I knew that only time would tell. In the meantime, I had to show him a better way by teaching him not to allow the shortcomings of others to prevent him from being the man he was called and chosen to be.

Not too long after that, our weekend visitations suddenly became nonexistent. Donnie, Jr., just seemed to be too busy with his friends and sports to come spend time with his father. He didn't even have time to play on the Sony PlayStation with me and talk with me through the night like we always did.

On the one hand, I understood that my son was now a growing teen and learning his independence. At the same time, I couldn't help but wonder if the church situation affected him worse than he was willing to admit and if he felt that I didn't properly handle the situation.

About a year went by. I had struggled every day to keep the lines of communication going with my son, but with no success. Meanwhile, other big things were going on in my life. I sold my home in Indiana and moved to North Carolina.

Even though the relationship between my son and me had already become nonexistent, it was difficult for me to think about leaving him behind. I knew that I was doing the right thing by moving to North Carolina, but I was also pretty sure that my move hurt him a lot. If nothing else, when he was ready to come back home again, I would no longer be close enough to pick him up for weekend visitations like I used to do.

Years passed. Despite my attempts to call and text my son, I hadn't heard from him. Then, finally, out of the clear blue sky, my phone rang.

It was Donnie, Jr.! He was drunk, angry, and hard-pressed to let me have it. He cussed me out and he told me that he was going to kick my a**!

I calmly listened to my seventeen-year-old son rant and rave. Finally, I asked him, "How exactly do you plan on making that happen?" After all, he was up in Ohio, and here I was down in North Carolina.

My son responded, "Give me your address, and I'll be right there!"

So, I did as he asked. I gave him my address, telling him that it was a ten-and-a-half-hour drive and to drive safely.

"I'll be waiting outside for you when you get here," I promised.

My plan was simple: get him to North Carolina, hug him, show him to his own room that he didn't even know I had already set up for him, and then tell him to sleep it off. We would hash things out together after he cooled down and got some rest from the long drive.

As it turned out, Donnie, Jr., never showed up, and it was the last time I heard from him. I went over and over that last conversation in my mind. It broke me to my very core.

I knew my son was hurt. In fact, I knew exactly how he felt, having felt exactly the same way when my father committed suicide. It was the all-too-familiar pattern of feeling abandoned, not wanted, and not good enough, leading directly to resentment. As for resentment, that has a way of creeping in on us unaware, at times lingering inside of us until it reaches the point of hatred and anger reveals its ugly face.

For me, I had no way of speaking to my dad after I felt abandoned by him. Because his decision was so final, I didn't even have a way to ask him questions in an effort to gain understanding about the choice he made.

In that sense, there was a huge difference between my father and me. I was still alive, which meant that I had the opportunity to set the matter straight with Donnie the Third. I had the opportunity to prove to my son how much I truly loved him.

The only things left to be determined were "when," "where," and "how" I would be granted the chance to discuss all those situations with him. I was bound to win my son's heart back one way or another!

Chapter Five

Enlightened by Truth

As I prepared for the days ahead I began to diligently seek out the Scriptures. It was through God's very Word of Truth that I was able to ready myself for the road that lay ahead.

I already knew that it was God alone Who created all things, both great and small. In reading and studying His Word, I was reminded that He is a God Who gives life and life more abundantly!

The Lord created families, including fathers, mothers, and children. He established the structure of a home, intending for it to be built upon a strong foundation and desiring that all of us live in love, unity, and peace as a family unit that can be likened to a kingdom on earth as it is in heaven.

There are many stories found in the Word of God that deal with difficult family issues. These accounts tell about truth, perseverance, faith, hope, loss, and love. They are true-life events about real people who suffered through some of life's greatest trials and tragedies.

Some stories are about families in turmoil who sought reconciliation. Others are about families who were torn apart by the schemes of the enemy, the same exact schemes we find extremely active in the days we live in today. After all, we live in a world full of confusion and chaos, a world full of broken families.

However, God, knowing full well what would become of the world after sin entered the picture, already developed a plan and a ministry for reconciliation. Thus, it was within His written Word that I was able to find the courage and determination I so desperately needed to confront the character flaws within myself to become the father I believed my children would desire.

In this particular season of growth, I had to be willing to take a look outside of my own box and see the bigger picture. When I did this, I saw that there was a much bigger problem going on within myself than a mere surface issue. I realized that I had an emotional problem, which cut deep for all parties involved.

What was this emotional issue? I was personally scarred by different events in the past, which resulted in parts of my heart becoming hardened. In many ways, I had become numb to the natural sensitivities that I needed to possess if I truly intended to be a man of understanding and win back the love and trust of my children.

Furthermore, my trust in others was gone in many ways, to the point where my faith and hope in humanity were hanging by a mere thread. To say the very least, my very outlook on life was bleak. This was not at all the type of attitude that I wanted to pass on to my children!

I knew that if there was any chance of reconciling with my kids, I had to change my perspective on life as a whole. The issues I dealt with were not visible to the naked eye because they were internal and deeply rooted matters of the heart. In other words, I was dealing with things that only God could see and fix. Only the Lord could bring healing and understanding to me throughout His process of renewing me from the inside out.

As I continued to study God's Word, I could see clearly throughout its pages that we are faced with a real enemy who seeks to rob, kill, and destroy us day in and day out. Satan especially targets families with one thought in mind: to destroy them by any means necessary. He uses spiritual attacks to tear apart families and tries to ruin what God initially created and called good!

The work of the enemy brings forth many serious consequences and ramifications for fathers, mothers, and children. From loss of time together to deep emotional hurt and pain, the destructive work shows up as a clear reflection in our individual characters. As hard as we might try to hide our deeply rooted family issues, it is extremely easy to spot and affects us deeply until we bravely face it and find the cure in God's healing power.

In any situation where a spiritual battle is going on, true wisdom and understanding are essential. As I learned, it's especially necessary to grasp what is going on in the bigger picture. Otherwise, we will feel like everything is outside of our control.

We may nearly drive ourselves crazy by trying to find a man made solution.

As I gained wisdom and understanding, I had to show my willingness to accept the things that had happened, all of which were truly beyond my control. Instead of handling them on my own, I needed to surrender all of these struggles over to God.

At that point, I knew that it was imperative that I gain even greater knowledge to not only understand what I had gone through but also to stop and consider what my children were still going through without me! Wisdom and knowledge go hand-in-hand, bringing forth insight and discernment. I desperately needed each of these virtues as I prepared to somehow reenter my children's lives.

Another absolutely essential thing was forgiveness, not only for those who sought to hurt me but even more so for myself. As I allowed God to work in my heart, forgiveness took the place of any lingering resentment that lay dormant within my heart. After all, two wrongs don't make a right. I had to be the bigger man in all things, knowing that my actions speak louder than words.

As I went through the healing and growing process, I saw that new and changed actions spoke volumes to the new man I was bound and determined to be. I was learning what true grace and mercy were all about and how to receive the understanding to live out these two gifts so that I could use them every day.

This whole process became a transformation that really started in my heart and changed my whole perspective. It actually goes against the very grain of what society teaches us. It is none other than a war of the spirit against the flesh, since our flesh prefers to react in haste and give very little thought to the long-term effects, instead of walking in this new life of grace and mercy.

A spiritual maturity began to unfold in me, replacing the negative and destructive behaviors that once held me down and kept me bound to thoughts of hopelessness. Playing the blame game was no longer a part of the equation. As a man and a father, it was my responsibility to take accountability for things that had gone wrong, even if they weren't my fault and were out of my control.

I began to see beyond all the nonsense of the past as I began to look at the bigger picture. My children's lives were at stake, revealing a far greater purpose for my existence. I could no longer just allow them to slip out of my life without telling them how much I truly loved them and always have. Picking and choosing my battles wisely became an asset that only proved to produce positive outcomes.

As I continued to seek out the Scriptures, I saw that God's plan for reconciliation extended far beyond His plan for us to merely be reconciled to Him. His love, His grace, His mercy, and His forgiveness are so much more, being given to us through His ministry of reconciliation so that we all might be reunited with one another. He desires that fathers, mothers, children, and whole families alike be brought back together!

I knew within my heart that if I had any chance of accomplishing my deep desire to reconcile with my children, God's way was the only way that would work. It began with a battle that had to be fought on the battlefield of faith, wrought in prayer, grounded in hope, and steadfast in love. This meant that I had to place my trust completely in the Lord and put all things within His guidance. Instead of trying to do things my way, I had to allow Him to make the necessary changes within me.

Even as I set out to act in faith, I found that it is not at all an easy thing to achieve. My flesh constantly warred against the ways of God. While it was always easy to cast blame on others, it was another thing to stop and take accountability for both my actions and the actions of others. Instead of repaying evil with evil, it was imperative that I respond with grace and mercy, regardless of the accusations that were thrown at me.

Every day, I had to stand my ground in the face of great opposition, declaring my position of possessing strength from within by having the ability to give forgiveness, even to those I felt did not deserve it. It was not at all an easy thing to achieve! Yet, it was absolutely necessary, proving to be beneficial to both me and others in the long run.

During this time of spiritual warfare, I thought back forty years to the days when I was young. I distinctly remembered a moment in time when both my parents came to my defense, showing me the importance of staying true to what they taught me to believe and, even more so, to be faithful to the God I came to know and love. I saw and received firsthand the value of having both of my parents in my life and the self-esteem it gave me as I sought to show God honor and glory in all things.

At the time, I was attending a quiet Catholic school tucked away deep within my neighborhood called Queen of Peace. The school staff was made up of priests and nuns who were highly respected by everyone in the community.

While learning at that school, I was taught that respecting a person's position was of the utmost importance. The nuns were to be called "Sister," followed by her first name, and the priests were to be called "Father," followed by his first name. All the students were taught to show this appearance of great respect to others in a position of higher authority, especially because these individuals were known as dedicated servants of God!

One night, I was reading my Bible at home in bed before falling asleep. I came across a Scripture verse in the very words of Jesus that read, "Call no man your father upon the earth: for One is your Father, which is in heaven" (Matthew 23:9).

I thought deeply about this verse, knowing that I was being taught something very different, and which actually went directly against Scripture. Even though I was only a young boy at the time, I felt a strong conviction to obey the Word of God instead of what I was being taught and made to say in the Catholic school system.

The more I thought about this verse, the more it weighed heavily upon my heart. What was I to do? How was I supposed to handle this, knowing that calling a respected man of the clergy by anything other than his professional title of "Father" was a sign of great disrespect?

The very next day, as I walked into school, I was greeted by my principal, "Father Clancy."

Father Clancy was a great man, highly respected by all his parishioners for being extremely active within the neighborhood. He genuinely loved people and sought to help anyone who called upon him. Not to mention, Father Clancy lived on the same street as me and would come out of the rectory at times to play sports with us kids and tell us stories on the weekend. Even my parents thought highly of him, having been close friends with him throughout the years.

That day, he greeted me, "Good morning, Donnie, how are you doing?"

I politely responded, "Good morning, Mr. Clancy, I'm doing great, thanks for asking. And how about you?"

The look that came across his face was one of deep concern, and he corrected me by saying, "You meant to say 'Father Clancy,' right?"

I looked back at him and said, "No, sir, I can no longer call you 'Father,' Mr. Clancy."

An astonished look came across his face. My answer had brought him such great surprise that he invited me into his office. Yes, I was being called into the principal's office!

Mr. Clancy then asked me to sit down and began to question me, wondering if I was feeling okay and wanting to know where this sudden form of disrespect was coming from.

I explained to him what I had read in the Bible only the previous night, words that I was sure he knew about and had read for himself while attending seminary.

Furthermore, I told Mr. Clancy that I couldn't wait to share my findings in religion class. I thought for sure that I had found a golden nugget and would receive a great response from my teacher and classmates. Plus, it would make for a truly deep discussion and bring us all into a greater understanding of Who God is as our Father. After all, we always started every morning by reciting the

"Our Father," a prayer we were taught to memorize.

Besides all that, I was confident that Mr. Clancy, of all people, would respect God's authority over my life. He would recognize my willingness to obey God's Word and encourage me in it, especially as a man of the cloth who understood the Scriptures on a deeper level than I did.

Unfortunately, none of my thoughts or hopes came to pass. In fact, I never even made it to class that day. Instead, he called my mother and instructed her to come pick me up and take me home, as I was now facing the threat of being expelled from school.

Once my mother heard the news of what I had said and done, she was shocked. In fact, she didn't know what to say, so she merely replied, "Thanks for calling me. My husband and I will have a discussion about this with Donnie, and we will be in touch with you as soon as we figure all this out."

Once I explained my strong convictions about the matter to my parents, they saw that I was correct. God's Word held precedence in our home above all things. Plus, they already knew that I had a special calling on my life and believed that this was just the beginning of things to come.

As my mother promised Mr. Clancy, a meeting was then scheduled. This time, both my parents went with me to the school, and we all sat in the principal's office together.

My parents then explained my thoughts and actions to Mr. Clancy. As I quietly sat beside them, I watched as his face took on a heavy look of regret and disappointment. He could tell that there was no way I was going to be made to call him "Father."

After my parents finished speaking, Mr. Clancy's recommendation was either to pull me out of the school quietly or to be prepared for me to face official expulsion. His reasoning was that such behavior would negatively affect both the other students and the Catholic church as a whole, since it would be viewed as disrespectful, disobedient, and downright treason. In other words, my behavior was not at all going to be tolerated.

This answer shocked my parents, and they looked at one another in amazement and disgust! Naturally, they didn't want the stigma of being expelled from school stamped on my academic records, especially when I had the courage to stand up for what I believed.

Needless to say, that ended my time of education in the Catholic school system. I was in the fourth grade at that time, so my parents figured out a way to send me to a local Christian academy. After all, they felt that they had no other choice because they wanted to keep me out of the public schools and had high hopes for my future.

Of course, my parents also began to look at the Catholic church differently. They couldn't believe that the whole church would take such extreme measures to protect the appearance of the institution while ultimately hurting a child's reputation in the process. Despite being a respected leader in the community, Mr. Clancy lost a lot of respect in the eyes of my parents that day.

I definitely needed to lean on both my father and my mother during that time. Despite the way that situation worked out, I was happy to have my parents to share my thoughts with and to be able to hear their opinions as well. I truly valued their presence and advice for my life, as they did their best to lead and guide me in the right direction.

The bigger lesson I learned in having come across that verse and dealing with that situation was that I saw how God Himself was serious about being a Father and the role that came with it. Fatherhood was a position that came with great responsibility and wasn't to be taken lightly.

I saw how He truly calls us to a higher standard of living, expecting men to be the exact representation of His character by telling us to lead our families in the way of righteousness and holiness. This could only be learned through patience, prayer, and studying His word. After all, the Lord is the greatest Teacher who walked the face of the earth.

Remembering that story only reinforced my quest to reconcile with my children. The only questions that remained to be answered were, "What kind of father would I turn out to be to my kids?" "Would I become the father I believed my children would desire, accepting me back into their lives?" "Had I become the father I always desired to be?"

While those answers hung in the balance, I continued to walk this process out in faith and hope for the best possible outcome. During the years of separation between me and my children, life didn't stop.

I met an amazing girl who worked at a home-less mission as the volunteer coordinator. It was a mission I frequented daily, ministering to those who sought refuge from homelessness. She and I hit it off almost immediately. We had a lot in common and shared the same heart for those who were without. We fell in love, got married, and continued to travel, reaching as many as we could to lend assistance to all different kinds of people in their times of need.

My prayer of finding true love had finally been answered. She was exactly what I had been praying for and has been nothing more than a blessing to me.

Four years later, we received some very exciting news: Liz was expecting! We were going to have a baby. While the news came as quite a shock to us, we were both excited and nervous at the same time. I was forty-seven and going to be a father again. The thought alone of being that old and knowing that I had been absent from my children's lives for so long gave me a lot to think about.

As we continued to travel, the days, weeks, and months seemed to fly by. The day had come, and the hour was here: Titus Michael Hardison was born, weighing in at eight pounds, three ounces and measuring twenty-one and a half inches long. He was bigger than life!

It truly is amazing what the life of a newborn can do when you first hear his cry and hold him in your arms. He was exactly what I needed, complete with blonde hair and beautiful blue eyes. He reminded me of my dad and my oldest son. My wife and I just adored him.

As young Titus became part of our daily lives, I often found myself thinking back to my oldest son, Donnie, Jr., and when he was just a newborn. I remembered him as a young boy and how he grew up into a teen, and I desperately missed both him and his sisters.

Within a few months, I was in the process of writing my first book, a memoir about my life titled *One Man's Journey: The Untold Story of the Quest for Truth*, which I successfully published on February 21, 2024. It was the story of my own life, as I grew from a young boy into a man, detailing many of the trials and tribulations that I both faced and overcame.

Even more importantly, it was a story of the legacy that I was carrying on from my parents, the heritage that I was passing on to my children. To that end, after my book was officially published, I ordered three hardcover editions and carefully personalized them by including pictures of me, each of my children, and their grandparents. I also wrote down my phone number and email address in case they wanted to contact me directly.

It was perfect: the book had everything I wanted to share with them and included an invitation, letting them know my door was open and had always been. From there, all that was left for me to do was to package each book individually and send them to the only addresses I knew—their mothers' houses—with the hopes that they would receive them.

Of course, I also hoped that each one of my children would call me after having read the book, but that decision was to be left completely up to them. I did believe that, whether good or bad, negative or positive, there is a price to pay for every decision made in life. I could only wonder what would happen next. Would reconciliation finally happen? Or had the damage already been done? Was there ever going to be a break in the silence between me and my children?

I had no idea what would come of my efforts. At the end of the day, all I knew was that I had done my best as a loving father and had to leave the results in the Lord's hands. I was ready to accept whatever lay ahead.

Chapter Six

A Break in the Silence

I t had been about a week since my wife and I mailed my book to my children. It was a week of waiting that felt like a whole year. We made sure to keep the tracking numbers so we could keep an eye on the three packages as they traveled across the country. Personally, I wanted to make sure that they were delivered.

The funny thing is, not everything works out as planned. My wife noticed toward the end of the week that while two of the packages had been delivered, the third one just happened to be misrouted and would be delivered a day later than originally expected. I couldn't help but wonder which one of the packages it was. I had no idea of knowing and realized that I just had to wait it out to see what would take place.

At the very least, with two books delivered and the last one still on its way, I was hoping to receive a call or an email from two of my children to let me know they had received my gifts. Still, I couldn't help but wonder how everything would turn out. As my wife and I had ongoing conversations about the matter, we often prayed together and asked that God's will be done. Only time would tell how everything would turn out.

By the next day, I still had not received any response from my children. As that morning and the afternoon crept by, my spirits began to tank, so I decided to take a nap and try to rest my mind.

This was not the time to lose hope! It was a time to practice patience while trusting in the Lord.

Many thoughts raced through my mind as I tried to reason with the lack of response. Perhaps my children wanted to read my book first before responding? Or perhaps life had them in a different location, and they had not physically received the book? I had no idea. Yet, I did know how news travels fast and phone calls would be made, making known the existence of my memoir among different family members and extended relatives.

Then there was the issue of the misrouted package. That one remaining book still left to be delivered had the ability to make one of my children feel left out and neglected. That was not at all what I wanted!

As these thoughts swirled through my mind, I did my best to push them away and let myself fall asleep instead. Just as I was finally entering a peaceful moment of rest, my phone began to ring.

Groggily, I looked at the screen and saw that the call was coming from a private number. I don't generally answer calls that come across as private, for the simple reason that it might be a spam call. Besides that, everyone that I know and talk to comes up with their name and photo. This time was different, however, and I had the sudden urge to answer the phone.

"Hello," I said.

The caller on the other end answered in like: "Hello."

Immediately taken off guard, I asked, "Who is this?"

With a touch of irony, the voice responded, "'Who is this?' he says!"

At that very moment, I knew exactly who it was. It was my son! With excitement in my voice, I replied, "DONALD MICHAEL!"

He chuckled and quickly got to the point. "So, I heard you wrote a book. Where's my copy?"

Everything I knew about the misrouted package suddenly clicked in my mind, and I scrambled to explain the whole scenario. I told him exactly what happened, gave him the tracking number, and explained that his book was set to be delivered the next day. Of course, I also apologized for the delay.

Once that was squared away, I asked him how he was doing and how he had been.

Donnie, Jr., went straight for it, sharing some very exciting news. "I'm getting married!" he said. "I met the girl of my dreams, and I'm a Christian!"

I was overtaken by excitement at the news and congratulated him. I was even granted the opportunity to speak with his fiancée, who was very pleasant on the phone. They both seemed very happy, and I could tell they were enjoying sharing these details about their lives and their future together with me. It was great, especially seeing how our conversation began with a positive start after having been separated by silence for so many years. My son was now twenty-seven and excited about his future. I couldn't have been happier for him.

As we continued to speak, the hard questions began to come to the surface. For example, Donnie, Jr., asked, "Why now? After all these years, why come back now?"

"A fair question," I said aloud, knowing that his perspective was one-sided on the matter as I thought back to his sudden disappearance when I was living back in Indiana. In response, I told him what was in my heart. "Why not now? While it's true we have missed out on a lot of time with each other, it's never too late to make amends and move forward."

Of course, I also had to mention how much I looked forward to catching up with him on the things that we both missed out on. I explained to my son how much I missed him and how much I had always desired to be a part of his life. I told him what I went through and how I felt about missing out on his high school years. I mentioned how I thought about him all the time.

In return, Donnie, Jr., said to me, "Life sure has a funny way of working things out, doesn't it?"

I couldn't have agreed with him more. As he continued to speak with me, I couldn't help but notice that we said a lot of the same things. In particular, he now used certain catchphrases that I would use on him when he was a kid. It was a very welcome encounter.

As my son and I continued to talk, we both understood that trust was something we had to reestablish with each other. Let's face it: once trust is broken, it's a hard thing to recover from.

So, I started by explaining to Donnie, Jr., that while trust was generally something earned and not given, I wanted to approach it differently than most would choose to do. After having said all that, I told my son that I wanted him to know that I was giving him my trust outright without him needing to earn it. What he did with my trust, however, was completely up to him.

My words took Donnie, Jr., by surprise, as I'm sure it would do the same for anyone. The thought of having me give him trust outright was a completely new concept for him. Although I could tell that he was trying to figure out my statement, he was also happy to hear it, as he told me that he really appreciated me telling him that.

Having come to the end of our conversation, I reminded him to track his package and that I would do the same, planning on emailing him to let him know when I received the delivery confirmation. You see, my son wasn't quite ready to give me his phone number just yet, but he provided me with his email and promised that he would give me his number in due time.

With all that being said, we closed out the talk by mentioning our hopes for the future. While we agreed that we didn't know what was in store, we knew that this day was a step in the right direction. We were both excited to have found each other once again and believed that the best was yet to come.

Immediately after getting off the phone, I told my wife all about our talk, who had been listening intently. She admitted to feeling a knot in the pit of her stomach over the whole encounter, hoping this turn of events wouldn't add any more hurt and pain to my life that had already been shadowed by so much tragedy. After all, she was well aware of the many battles and tribulations I had already faced and overcome, and her heart has always been one of true love, compassion, and protection for me.

Yet, knowing my desire to reconcile with my children, my wife was there to support and honor me, no matter what the outcome might be. As for what the future would hold, we both knew that only time would tell and were determined to take each day as it came, while doing our best to live in love for one another and for any of my children who chose to reenter my life.

The next morning, I received the expected delivery confirmation that my son's book had finally made it, so I emailed him to let him know.

Come to find out, Donnie, Jr., knew about the book's location, having already picked it up from his mother's house. He mentioned that he planned on reading it and would be in touch after he did so.

With that, I simply had to wait to hear back from him. To say the least, I was both excited and nervous to hear my son's thoughts about my book.

About six hours later, Donnie, Jr., called, having spent the whole day reading *One Man's Journey* from start to finish. I was surprised to hear of his marathon reading session, but I was even more eager to know his thoughts.

My son started out by saying, "I read your book, and I think it's really good. I get it, you're out to change the world for the better. I think it's a beautiful thing. Thank you for sharing it with me. It helps."

I waited, wondering if he had more to say. As expected, Donnie, Jr., went on, "If I might add, I was a little disappointed that you didn't write more about me in it."

Of course, that only gave me the opportunity to share with him my plan to one day write a book about us, dedicating it to him. That idea alone made him happy, knowing I had a well-thought-out plan for the days ahead.

As we continued to talk, I could tell that reading my book had done a lot of good for my son. If nothing else, it reassured him of the father he once knew me to be. Not only that, but my story gave him something to be proud of since he was able to share it with his fiancée and her family, who also found my story fascinating.

Over the next couple of weeks, my son and I continued to talk by email and phone. I came to see that my promptness in responding to his phone calls was greatly important to him. Essentially, it was his way of testing me and rebuilding the trust in me to keep our relationship going forward.

One night, as I was finishing up dinner for the family, my phone rang. I was just in the act of pulling a hot pan of homemade lasagna out of the oven, which prevented me from answering the call.

As soon as my hands were free, I looked to see who the missed call had been from. Seeing the familiar private number designation, I immediately knew it was my son. I felt a sinking feeling, knowing how much that phone call meant to him and that I had no way of calling him back.

At that very moment, I received an email alert. It was from Donnie, Jr., and he sounded upset.

"I tried to call you, but you didn't answer!" the message read.

I instantly replied, telling my son that I was now free to talk if he wanted to call me back.

The phone rang once again, and this time I was able to answer. My son immediately began to share his thoughts with me on how he felt when I did not answer when he called.

In return, I told Donnie, Jr., that not having his number left me without the option to call him back and forced me to rely only on his email for communication. I further explained to him that he was placing unrealistic demands on me. Like him, I had a life and family to take care of as well.

As we continued to talk, he thought about what I said. By the end of our conversation, my son decided that he was finally ready to give me his number. With that, we both recognized that our trust in each other had reached a very important milestone, one where the door to communication was able to flow in two directions instead of just one.

As each day and each conversation passed by, Donnie, Jr., and I grew closer together. We experienced the need to have each other back in our lives, which also included knowing that we had each other to lean on for advice and help if that time ever arose. We especially enjoyed conversing, cracking jokes, and laughing together. It was great.

Finally, we came to the point where it was time to visit in person. Of course, I had already brought it up weeks earlier in normal conversation, inviting my son and his fiancée to come visit us for a free weekend or week trip, whatever they were interested in and comfortable doing. Yet, I knew that I had to wait for my son to make his own decision in his own time.

One day, Donnie, Jr., asked me, "So, when are you planning to come up to see me? I'd like to formally introduce you to my fiancée and give you the chance to get to know her before she becomes a part of the family." Plus, my son was also eager to meet his baby brother, who was still an infant but growing by leaps and bounds every day.

My son's invitation made me very happy. At the time, my wife and I were in eastern North Carolina, a ten-hour drive to his location in northern Ohio. So, I told him that his idea sounded great and that my wife and I would talk and then let him know what would work for us.

After talking through the possibilities with my wife, I called Donnie, Jr., and told him that we had decided to make the trip in a few weeks. We knew it would take a couple of days to get up to Ohio and suggested a weekend visit to Columbus, which would shorten our drive by a few hours and not interfere with my son's work schedule. He readily agreed, and the plan was set.

The weeks leading up to the trip seemed to fly by. Both my son and I were extremely excited about the upcoming visit, knowing that we were finally going to see each other again after many years.

Before I knew it, my family and I were on the road, on our way up north. I was excited to finally see my little boy again. This time, however, he wasn't a boy any longer. Instead, he was a man who had worked through his own trials and tribulations and was learning more about what it meant to have his own life every day.

I had a lot to ponder on during the drive, but most of all, I hoped for a beautiful reunion, a time of healing, and a time of bonding. Once again, I knew that only time would tell. Yet, I also knew that my prayers were being answered—one step at a time, one person at a time, and one day at a time.

CHAPTER SEVEN

AT FIRST GLANCE: THE REUNION

While texts, emails, and phone conversations are great, there is a lot to be said about face-to-face time spent together. Personal encounters hold a huge significance in the well-being of a human's life, physically, mentally, and emotionally.

I had been hoping for this moment for my son and me for a very long time. I had even been preparing myself for it, even while not fully knowing if this day would ever come. I could see that my prayers were being answered, yet I could only wonder what the future had in store, both for myself and for my entire family in my quest to make our family whole again.

The drive took me, Liz, and Titus a couple of days, and Donnie, Jr., and I communicated the entire way. He and I were excited about seeing each other again, looking forward to spending time together. Plus, my son also has a very protective spirit about him, so he wanted to make sure our travels were safe and sound.

Upon arriving in Columbus, we had planned the trip perfectly so that Donnie, Jr., was just ten minutes behind us. It gave me a chance to look around our weekend Airbnb, unpack the car, and get Liz and Titus situated.

As I was grabbing the last of our luggage from the trunk of the car, out of my peripheral vision,

I noticed a black car with Ohio plates pulling up behind me. It was Donnie, Jr., and his fiancée.

At the first glance of my son, I caught a huge smile beaming across his face. That's another thing that my son and I both possess—our infectious smiles, a dead giveaway to how we are feeling in the moment. It only lasted for just a moment, however, since he immediately tried to contain his expression. After all, he was never one to show emotions in front of others.

I set down my bags momentarily and approached my son. We gave each other a big hug, and he proudly introduced his beautiful bride-to-be to me. She was also excited about the weekend ahead and couldn't have been happier to meet her man's dad, wife, and baby brother.

After all the introductions were made, I was happy to see that everything felt very natural and that everyone seemed to bond together almost immediately. Liz and I made sure that the young couple settled in comfortably, and then I noticed that my son needed a haircut and a shave.

So, I told him, "Son, you're getting a haircut and a shave by yours truly."

He looked at me a bit curiously and asked, "Do you know how to fade and properly line me up?"

I responded, "Absolutely! Cutting hair is something I do a lot to help others out."

"Thank God!" Donnie replied with a grin.

My guess was that it was something that he had wanted to get done for a while, but he just didn't have the time to do it between his work and other responsibilities.

Either way, I was glad my fatherly instincts kicked in. I've always been big on appearance, knowing you never get a second chance to make a first impression. Not to mention, I know what a fresh haircut and a clean shave can do for a man's self-esteem.

It didn't take long to finish up the haircut and shave. After a quick shower to freshen up, Donnie, Jr., was ready to show off his new look. He couldn't have been happier with my skills, and his fiancée was impressed to see her man looking like the handsome guy she met and fell in love with.

From there, it was time for the young couple to surprise us. They came bearing presents, which was an extremely thoughtful act of kindness that I wasn't expecting at all. For Titus, they brought a beautiful, illustrated children's Bible and some stuffed animals. They fell in love with him at first sight and nicknamed him "Tiny T," a name that suits him well and has stuck to this day, no matter how big he is.

For Liz, they brought a lovely, flowered mug inscribed with a Scripture verse that read, "With God All Things Are Possible." It was a sign to both of us, making it crystal clear that God had heard my prayers and was truly answering them.

My hopes and desires to reconcile with my family were taking place right before our very eyes!

As for dear old Dad, I got a coffee mug with a Bible verse from the Psalms that read, "My Cup Runneth Over." This gift spoke volumes to me, reminding me how important it was to both my son and me that we had finally reconnected. Honestly, it was exactly how I had been feeling since we first spoke on the phone. To this day, it's the only mug I use for my morning coffee, giving me a sense of pride and reminding me of how thankful and grateful I am for my son's presence in my life.

As our weekend continued, we all spent a lot of time getting to know each other. Donnie, Jr., and I also took the opportunity to catch up and have deep conversations about the different situations we had endured along life's greatest journey.

Some of our conversations were heartbreaking to me. Each time something new came up, I listened intently to my son, quietly thinking to myself that

I wished I had been able to be there for him in his time of need. Donnie had been through a lot and had seen a lot. He learned from experience that life doesn't always deal you a winning hand. He had come to learn how unpredictable and messy life really was.

For example, my son told me how the ones he used to call his friends were no longer close to him. This came as quite a surprise to me since I personally knew the guys he was talking about. They all went to school together, played football together, and even came to my house and spent the weekends with us during Donnie's visitations. They were good kids who were very respectful and full of jokes, adding a lot of laughter to the house that I truly appreciated and enjoyed.

Donnie also told me that the ones he used to trust and look up to only ended up letting him down. These were the people he had gone to in search of advice and encouragement in my absence. He now wholeheartedly knew the truth of the matter that people come in and people go out of our lives for many different and unexpected reasons.

While the loss of connections hurt him, Donnie always pressed on while seeking to figure things out. I couldn't believe the similarities we had in our lives, mirroring each other in more ways than I could count. Although I didn't understand why things had to happen this way, I was grateful to understand where he was coming from. Having been there myself time and time again, it allowed me to speak with my son on many different levels. I also knew that he would fully comprehend where I was coming from as well, which would bring him greater insight into the questions that still lingered in his mind.

Donnie also shared more of the story about him and his fiancée with me, mentioning how meeting her made all the difference in his life. He talked with me about how he once felt unlovable, not good enough, and totally beaten down by the things he was left to endure on his own. I knew the feeling all too well, as I had been left to feel the same way after having lost my parents. We both agreed that we'd never wish that dark place in life on any person because of it being such an extremely hard thing to face and overcome.

My son went on to say how finding his fiancée touched him deeply, changing his outlook and perspective on life in a very profound way. He had found trust again as well as a reason and purpose to live. As I heard all this, I felt very grateful to hear about all the ways that Donnie was healing from his own struggles in the past. Instead of allowing his pain to fester into resentment and bitterness, he was seeking the way of love and forgiveness.

These conversations led to a sensitive topic that my son wanted to bring up with me. He told me that there was another thing that we had both experienced on the same level. It was something deep and not at all an easy subject to talk about.

From there, Donnie began to refer back to my story of how I had attempted suicide. "I get it," he said, going on to further elaborate on how he understood the deep despair that I had been facing because of what he also had gone through some years back.

As I continued to listen, my heart broke, hearing my son explain that he also took an attempt on his own life. He had been found just in the nick of time with a rope around his neck that was tied to a door. At the time, Donnie had come to a very dark place and no longer wanted any part of his life.

After hearing this story, I was immediately awash in a deep feeling of respect and gratitude for the man who saved my son's life. I was thankful above all that someone was there for Donnie in his time of great need.

At the same time, as his father and the very one who brought him into this world, it was still heartbreaking and shocking to hear the story. Having been there myself at one point in my life, I realized that it's one thing to be well-acquainted with that place of utter despair, but it's a totally different thing to know your own child has faced it as well.

It took every bit of composure I had inside of me to keep from crying in front of my son! I wanted to maintain a spirit of strength and continued hope for him, but there was no way of completely hiding the fact that his story deeply affected me. As we continued to talk, Donnie could tell how much compassion I had for him in his time of deep darkness. Both of us were simply grateful to have each other back in our lives once again.

I continued to reflect on my son's story long after we talked about it. I couldn't help but think about the many people I had met whose stories turned out very differently, ending in the loss of their child or their parent. Having dealt with the aftermath of my father's suicide, I knew firsthand the kind of trauma it held over my life as a survivor.

If nothing else, remembering these things deepened my desire to do what I could to prevent others from facing such tragedy in their own families. I knew that the message of love had to be shared with as many people as possible. I wanted each person ever faced with hopelessness to realize that they were never alone but actually wanted and loved by One who was greater than the deepest darkness.

Meanwhile, the weekend in Columbus continued to go well. My wife, being born with a spirit of hospitality, made sure that everyone was comfortable and well-fed. Even though Liz is quiet by nature, her presence is felt through gentleness, kindness, and love. She especially enjoyed seeing all of us talk deeply about matters of the heart, knowing that this was not just a coincidence but a divine appointment intended to restore a family that was once broken.

She also took to Donnie as if he were her own son and welcomed his fiancée's company in the kitchen while they cooked delicious meals together. Liz saw in Donnie a lot of the same traits that were in me—charm, charisma, and true compassion for others. There was no doubt about it, Donnie, Jr., was definitely his father's son! Liz now had two Donnies in her life, which she welcomed with open arms.

Besides the many conversations, we played games together. It was another way of interacting with each other in a more lighthearted way, bringing laughter to the house and showing our fun sides to each other. All in all, it was a delightful visit.

As our weekend was quickly coming to an end, I felt as if I needed more time with my son. Of course, my wife and I intended to return for their wedding if invited, but that was still months away. The weekend was a great one, but Sunday morning was just a sunrise away, and we both would be heading off in opposite directions.

My son, feeling the same way that I did, came to me and asked if I would be willing to come up to his area for a while. He wanted more time with us as well, but he used the convenient excuse that they needed help with all their wedding plans in the days ahead. Donnie explained that although he had to work, he would appreciate knowing I was nearby and would spend as much time with us as possible.

Speaking it over with my wife and seeing that we had the flexibility because of working remotely, we agreed, which made the two newlyweds-to-be extremely happy. So, it was settled. All my wife and I had to do was find a place where we could all find solace while enjoying one another and helping them prepare for their big day ahead.

Who would have thought that this first glance in a moment in time and space would have brought so much healing to everyone involved? While that which lay ahead was obviously unknown to us at the time, we all knew that it was worth seeking out.

As for me, I couldn't help but wonder what other encounters were in store for us in the coming weeks and months. I was curious to see how many other lives my wife and I would come to meet and positively affect in the days ahead. Although we had no idea what was coming next, we knew that the time we had just spent reconnecting with my son was a positive first step in the right direction.

We had started by creating new memories that would last a lifetime. After all, building relationships was something that my wife and I always had in common. We highly valued every act of empathy and did our best to practice love, compassion, and hospitality within our home every chance we got.

CHAPTER EIGHT

CLEAR LAKE

As we took the two-hour drive up to northern Ohio, we decided to stay at a hotel for a couple of days to give us time to find a long-term Airbnb. As a bonus, the hotel was only a couple of blocks away from where my son currently lived.

Just after we arrived and got settled in, Donnie, Jr., called to invite us over to meet his fiancée's family. Her mother and grandparents had already heard all about how our weekend went and couldn't have been happier for Donnie that he was finally able to reconnect with his dad.

The whole family was warm, welcoming, and ever so eager to get to know us more, having already fallen in love with my son for the man that he is. I was especially happy to see how every person showed great respect for Donnie, as he was always ready to meet each need with a willing and helpful hand. I saw how he had built some strong relationships with these people who now adored him and accepted him into their family.

Meanwhile, my wife found us a long-term Airbnb, a beautiful cottage nestled on Clear Lake close to the Indiana line, about an hour away from where my son lived. It was the perfect place to enjoy family weekend get-togethers—the lake, bonfires, and burgers on the grill.

Donnie, Jr., couldn't have been happier to hear the news. It kept all of us in close proximity to each other, allowing all of us to travel back and forth as needed. It also helped me and Liz be available to help the young couple finalize their plans for the big day ahead. We were all so happy to have the cottage on the lake as the perfect getaway from the stressful moments that life often comes with.

Everything was working out smoothly, and time seemed to be flying by, to say the least. We did our best to make the most of our time together, knowing their wedding day was only a couple of months away and we had no time to waste.

Visiting churches, checking out reception halls, and getting Donnie's tuxedo fitting taken care of topped the list, and of course, many other smaller details went into planning a big wedding. Throughout it all, it was important for Donnie to have his father there during these moments.

As all these things were being taken care of, our weekends were spent sharing quality time together—telling stories, laughing at jokes, playing games, and don't forget sharing favorite family recipes like Dad's Famous Deep-Fried Tacos!

Our time spent together in the months leading up to the big wedding day proved to be extremely valuable to both my son and his fiancée. They had an outlet to share their thoughts and feelings. They felt heard and understood while, as Donnie puts it, "having real talks," without fear of being shut down or being forced into a position where they felt judged. To them, our conversations were happening on a whole other level, ones that they looked forward to having, as we all set out together to find the answers to the many questions life seems to throw at us.

As May approached, we were all excited because we had two birthdays coming up to celebrate. Both my son and I are May babies and are only eighteen days apart from each other. Plus, it was the first time in many years that we would be able to celebrate them together.

As one can imagine, it brought me great excitement to prepare a special day for Donnie, Jr. My wife and I were especially looking forward to taking him to a bistro for a five-star birthday dinner.

I also came to find out that my son had never been to a concert before, and it just so happened that one of his favorite bands was going to be in town. So, we purchased tickets for the evening, telling Donnie, Jr., and his fiancée to go enjoy the special event together. I would have gone along with my son, but his choice of music is different from mine and completely out of my wheelhouse. Let's face it, it's a generational difference!

As his big day came closer, Liz also made a chocolate cake with vanilla frosting for him, decorating it with Jolly Ranchers, his favorite candy. Donnie, Jr., loved it, and it put a huge smile on his face to know the time and care that she put into everything on his behalf.

It was great to have finally spent my son's birthday with him, rather than remembering the day without him present and wishing the whole time that we were together, which was something I did every year I was without him.

My birthday was also spent with my son as we began to write this new chapter of reconciliation into our lives. Mine, however, was simple and exactly what I requested—a nice homemade meal, time spent around the evening campfire, and most importantly, my family being together again and having a good time. It was one of the best birthdays ever, full of memories that I will forever cherish.

As the days drew closer to my son's wedding day, Donnie felt the need to tell his family and friends that we had reconnected, wanting them to know that I would be attending the big event. We both knew that there would be those who would be happy for him and those who would give him opposition.

As he sought my advice on the matter, I told my son that his decision to tell whom he wanted to tell was completely up to him. I assured him that no matter what choice he made, I would stand behind it. After all, he was a man now, and I saw that this choice of his just showed his integrity in always wanting to do the right thing.

Having made his decision, Donnie, Jr., spoke to those he intended to tell. As expected, he was met with a mix of responses—some positive, some negative, and many types of questions in between.

As for the questions, the biggest one he had to answer was, "Why now?" His answer to them was bold and simple: "Because I believe in forgiveness," leaving them with that thought and then going on about his business.

For those who wanted to bring negativity, Donnie also made it clear that he wanted no drama at his wedding between everyone who was invited. This was a day for many to come together as family and friends to celebrate the happy couple as they took their vows before God in holy matrimony. It was a day where their lives would change forever, so they especially wanted it to be a day for the history books, one that would be built upon great memories to last a lifetime.

When Donnie, Jr., told me about his interactions, I saw that his answer about forgiveness would leave anyone thinking about their motives for asking the initial question in the first place. I was proud of him, and I was happy that he also felt good about what he had both done and said.

As the wedding plans continued, one of the most important things that the couple wanted was for God to be a part of their marriage. Liz and I were honored when they asked us to help them write a special piece for their celebration that started with prayer and continued with a unity ceremony called "The Three Cord Strand."

During the ceremony, three different colored strands of cord were braided together, unifying the Lord, the husband, and the wife together as one, showing the couple's commitment to the Lord and to one another. It was a beautiful idea that we loved being a part of and helping to plan, especially as we saw the excitement in their eyes as everything was gradually becoming a reality they could see and picture for their big day.

As we finally entered the month of July, one of the last major things to take care of was teaching my son how to dance. Well, it's not that he didn't know how to dance at all; it was just that this particular dance wasn't any old dance. This was a special waltz, the very first number that they would dance to as soon as they were officially introduced as Mr. and Mrs. Hardison at the reception.

Donnie was pretty excited to learn the waltz, already knowing that he had two left feet when it came to the slow and formal dance style. His fiancée was equally excited to have my help and to make her dream for their first dance as a married couple a reality.

Night after night, they practiced. With each attempt, they came closer to finding their perfect stride and flow. It was beautiful to watch them learn together, as I stood close by to help them correct and perfect their moves.

The last few weeks seemed to fly by. We shared many more moments with the couple as the days passed, enjoying their company and doing our best to love and support them as they were ready to navigate life on their own as husband and wife.

With everything for the wedding slowly falling into place, Donnie asked me when I planned on writing another book. Having enjoyed my first memoir, he encouraged me to write the next one, which I took as a huge compliment from my own son.

I had already been deep in thought about another possible book and mentioned it to him a while back, especially saying that I hoped to write about our journey together as father and son.

This time, Donnie, Jr., was curious to know more about my premise for writing the next book. So, I explained to him my thoughts and prayers about reconciliation and the hope it could offer families, parents, and children everywhere.

With that, my son looked at me and told me to write it. He gave me his blessing, seeing the greater importance and how our story could give hope to all those who had been estranged from each other, either as parents or children.

Having gotten his approval, I began to think long and hard about this new writing journey I was about to embark on. I couldn't have been more excited, knowing the potential the book possessed. Even more than that, I was thrilled to know that my son, even in the midst of planning for his big day, also wanted to be a part of changing this world and making it a better place.

Of course, I had very little time to reflect on the big picture with the wedding only a couple of days away. I needed much more time to think about everything, especially the great moments that had taken place between my son and me within such a short amount of time.

After all, I knew that when the big day was upon us, life once again was going to change, sending us off in two opposite directions. Yet, this time, my son and I had developed an even greater bond, sealed with a promise to be there for one another. Better yet, we not only stood in the roles of father and son but were also two men who sought to encourage one another during both the good times and the bad times. Best of all, we were two men who shared the same desire to see the same goodness in others as was seen within us as well.

CHAPTER NINE

SILENCE BREAKS THE HEART

Silence holds the power to accomplish great and many different things. When taking time within its realm, we find ourselves able to think and reflect on everything that is taking place inside us and around us. It can be a place of peace and solitude, or it can be a place of utter despair and agony. Truth be told, it can be both simultaneously.

During my times of silence and reflection, I always invite the Lord into my thoughts. I share with

Him all the things I'm thinking about and how I'm feeling. It's my alone time with Him, allowing me to not only tell Him what's in my heart but also hear directly from Him. It's my time to think, my time to pray, and my time to listen.

As I've taken the time to reflect throughout my life, I've seen many times that I'm offering my broken heart to the Lord. I've also come to learn that a broken heart isn't necessarily a bad thing. While it is extremely painful at times, there is a lot I've learned throughout the healing process.

Looking back and seeing the many seasons I've endured thus far, I've noticed that it's normal for seasons to come and for seasons to go. As the Word of God says in Ecclesiastes 3:1-8,

"To every thing there is a season, and a time to every purpose under the heaven:

A time to be born, and a time to die; a time to plant, and a time to pluck up that which is planted;

A time to kill, and a time to heal; a time to break down, and a time to build up;

A time to weep, and a time to laugh; a time to mourn, and a time to dance;

A time to cast away stones, and a time to gather stones together; a time to embrace, and a time to refrain from embracing;

A time to get, and a time to lose; a time to keep, and a time to cast away;

A time to rend, and a time to sew; a time to keep silence, and a time to speak;

A time to love, and a time to hate; a time of war, and a time of peace."

Throughout these emotional seasons, I've lived, I've loved, and I've lost. I have also gained so much knowledge and understanding in the midst of all of these seasons. Each time I spent a new season in silence before the Lord, I have been able to find healing on many different levels. For example, I realized that I no longer had to carry different burdens that haunted me from the past, something that I call the cross of deep regret, which is an unbearable cross to bear.

Another important piece of knowledge that I gained was understanding that life isn't an easy journey. In fact, life isn't supposed to be easy. Every trial, every tribulation, every setback, and every broken heart is an opportunity for us to grow and mature. It's essentially an opportunity to be enlightened by the truth, an opportunity that I've been given to live my best life.

Of course, each time I was in a difficult part of life, it certainly may not have felt like a great opportunity to me at first. However, I would soon realize that everything happens for a reason and that nothing happens just by chance.

During the times I sat in the silence of my thoughts, the Lord would begin to speak to me and remind me of every prayer I had ever prayed. My prayers have always been spoken from my heart, not only for myself but for so many others. I've prayed for people I know and for people I didn't know. I've especially prayed for my children.

I knew that since I hadn't been there physically for my children, I had no way to watch over them, to protect them, to guide them, to correct them, and to love them. It was as if I were a ghost, and the memory of my existence merely lingered in the hearts of my children from time to time. I wondered to myself if they still remembered the good times we had shared or if their thoughts of me had changed negatively due to my absence.

Then I thought back to how my mother had placed me and my life in the hands of God before she passed, asking Him to watch over me and guide me. I knew firsthand what that kind of prayer was able to accomplish.

I had no choice but to do the same for my children, knowing that God was the only One who was able to teach me how to navigate life on my own with the heartbreak I was experiencing. Only He could teach me how to become a better man today than I was yesterday, which included being the father that I truly desired to be. He showed me how to surrender to His will as He answered all my questions of "how," "what," "where", "when," and "why" all in His good time!

During the moments of quiet prayer and reflection, the Lord taught me that He had not only heard each of my requests for my children but that He was hard at work answering them. He helped me let go of the things I had no control over. He even showed me how to forgive those who were hellbent on hurting me and my family.

The Lord taught me not to repay evil with evil and how to hold my peace. This was not always an easy lesson for me, but it was one of the steps I needed to learn to gain true wisdom and understanding. "Even a fool, when he holdeth his peace, is counted wise: and he that shutteth his lips is esteemed a man of understanding" (Proverbs 17:28).

The Lord also showed me the power that can be found in the midst of silence. He reminded me of this very thing in Exodus 14:14, "The Lord shall fight for you, and ye shall hold your peace."

In His Word, He proved to me His power and His promise that He was truly with me and fighting for me. In that sense, as I allowed the Lord to work on me, He was actually busy working on my behalf and in my situation.

The Lord then made it ever so clear to me as He said in His loving and gentle voice, "What I've done for you, I will do for your children and for all those who call upon My Name."

As I heard this within the silence, peace came over me. That peace consumed my entire being as the Lord revealed to me my son's heart and how Donnie truly wanted to walk in a relationship with Him.

Memories came back to me from days in the past, and I could clearly see how the Lord kept Donnie's feelings from being hurt by the church situation years ago, which could have easily turned him away from Him when he was a young teen.

The Lord also showed me how the generational curse of suicide had been broken, not only over my life but over my son's life as well. He revealed my son's heart to me and how Donnie, Jr., no longer wanted to hold onto resentment, knowing the heavy burden of bitterness he had been carrying was only adding to depression and misery—two things we have all dealt with at some point in our lives.

I could see how Donnie came to find out for himself that forgiveness was so much easier to carry, bringing him resolve and peace in the matters he struggled with. I already knew that his heart had always been one that wanted to do the right thing. My son truly wanted happiness instead of misery, and his happiness always came from making others happy.

The Lord then showed me that, even in my absence, He had been and will always be there with Donnie, Jr., just as He has always been there for me. He showed me how my son, who was once a little boy and had now become a man, was now a man of integrity in his own right and in his own way. Just like me, Donnie had gone through a lot of hardships in his own life. He had been given the opportunity to learn and grow from each one of his situations as well.

In thinking about all of these things, I realized that the similarities my son and I share go beyond the personality traits that are easily spotted by outsiders. Both of us possess natural charisma and positivity that draw others to us like a magnet. Yet, the life lessons we've endured and learned from have brought forth far greater men in us than we could have ever imagined that we would be. Needless to say, I couldn't be prouder of the man Donnie, Jr., has become and is becoming each and every day!

One of the most important things that the Lord revealed to me during this time was that while the enemy had been busy breaking families apart, Jesus already had a plan of action in place to overcome and defeat each form of brokenness in places where it looked most hopeless.

In fact, it is through the Lord's ministry of reconciliation that hope and forgiveness are given a chance to take place. This ministry sets forth to reconcile and reconnect us with the ones we love and miss, bringing our families back together again.

I realized many different things throughout this entire process of facing silence, enduring brokenness, listening to the Lord, and accepting the lessons I needed to learn. Most of all, I understood that a heart that is broken is a heart twice saved from the pits of despair.

In the silence of it all, a transformation is taking place. This is none other than a transformation of strength, as your old heart is now replaced with a new one, a spiritual encounter that can only be defined as divine.

CHAPTER TEN

RECONCILIATION BEGINS WITH HOPE AND A PRAYER

The wedding day was finally upon us. The morning unexpectedly brought with it some challenges, but we dealt with each one in turn.

It all started with an early morning phone call alerting us that the power at the church was out, preventing the bridal party from getting ready. Liz and I immediately began to investigate the issue. I reached out to someone at the church to ask if they could provide us with more information about when the power would be restored, while Liz jumped online to check for any regional electrical problems.

As it turned out, there was a power outage in the area, and the crews were already on scene to work on the issue. It was a problem that couldn't be anticipated or hurried, but the power came back some time later, and plans went on as normal.

Meanwhile, Liz, Titus, and I prepared to arrive at the church earlier than originally planned, just in case other unexpected surprises happened. I was happy to be there for both my son and his fiancée, knowing that my mere presence to potentially handle any more situations would bring them peace of mind and make all the difference in the world for them.

We showed up at the church an hour and a half before the wedding and made it a point to go and see both the bride and groom in turn as they each made their own preparations for the ceremony. All the little details were being taken care of, and the clock was continually ticking away. I was happy to be there for my son from the sidelines, as he was now only a few short minutes away from the big moment.

The guests were all seated, the groom and his party took their positions at the front, and everyone waited for the ceremonial walk toward the altar. As the music began to play and the wedding procession began, my heart and my thoughts couldn't fully believe what was about to take place.

After years of missing my son and desiring to be in his life, God had done the impossible! There I was, taking part in one of the most important days of his life.

The groom and the bride were now standing before us, hand-in-hand with their eyes locked upon
each other. They began to share their vows that
they had personally written from their hearts for
each other. It was a touching moment that was
soon followed by what they considered to be the
most sacred part of their wedding service: "The
Three Cord Strand."

This ceremony involved braiding three differently colored cords together, symbolizing the new
bond between husband, wife, and God. The dark
brown strand was for the groom, showing his love
for his new bride. The light brown strand was
for the bride, standing for her love for her man.
The white strand was for God, representing His
purity, and it was placed in the middle of the other
two strands to symbolize how He was and always
would be at the center of their marriage.

As the minister spoke into their lives, he reminded the couple that love was stronger when lov-

ing God first. He instructed them to keep the three-cord strand within their home to regularly remind them of the foundation God brought to their lives, first separately as individuals and now together as they were united as husband and wife in holy matrimony.

The minister continued, saying, "Submit to one another out of reverence for Christ, as the Bible commands. Husbands, love your wives just as Christ loved the church and died for her, for Ephesians tells us that Christ gave himself up for the church, to make her holy. Give yourself to your wife and to your marriage fully, honor her, and honor this covenant. And wives, love your husbands with a gentle heart. Let him lead your family well as he strives to walk closely with Christ."

He then spoke to all the people witnessing the ceremony: "Let us all remember this day and celebrate the joy and love that God has put into these two hearts and the happy life that lies ahead of them."

With that being said, the marriage was sealed—not only with a kiss but with a covenant between them and God. As the newlyweds proceeded back down the aisle, everyone applauded in celebration, and tears were also falling in light of the excitement and emotion of the occasion.

The new couple exited the double doors with huge smiles on their faces to be greeted by a great cloud of shimmering bubbles blown by all of the guests. They were soon on their way to the reception hall to further celebrate their big day.

Upon their grand entrance, they were now formally and officially introduced as Mr. and Mrs. Donald Hardison! They walked hand-in-hand to the dance floor and began to move to the steps of the waltz that they had practiced and perfected together.

It was a wonderful sight to behold, and it took everything I had to keep myself from bawling like a baby. As I sat there, watching them take their first steps together as husband and wife, I recognized it as a beautiful moment of the love and unspeakable joy they had found within each other that was now captured in my memory.

The memory was even more precious to me because I knew that my time left to celebrate with them was coming to an end within only a few short hours. We had spent almost every day for the last several months together, bonding as a family, and it had been a powerful time of reconciliation.

After we said our farewells to the newlyweds, many thoughts flashed through my mind as we walked through the hallway toward the parking lot. I knew that although we both were heading off in two opposite directions, this time, it would be different for us. We now had a new family member, and all the memories we had just built together were a symbol and a promise of the beautiful life to come in the days ahead.

As I was heading out the door, I heard my son's once young voice say to me in a whisper, "I believe in forgiveness. Thank you so much for being here for me on one of the most precious days of my life. I love you, Dad, and I'll see you soon."

Conclusion

A Conversation with God

This story is just one example of what reconciliation can look like between family members. Of course, there are still others in my heart whom I desire to connect with and have as a regular part of my life. While that hasn't happened just yet, that is okay. I remain hopeful, knowing that my door has been and will always be open until my dying day.

In that sense, this book might not end with the biggest of red bows, but it should remind all of us that the ministry of reconciliation is always a work in progress. Letting go of the past things that have hurt us and haunted us isn't always an easy thing to do, yet it is imperative and an important part of the process. If you are searching for healing and hope for better days, finding forgiveness is the best way to start.

It's never too late to make amends. You can still become that special person in the life of your absent parent. There is always hope for you and the child that you have lost out on time with. Putting forth the work to reach that point isn't at all easy, but it comes with a far greater reward than one could ever imagine.

My hope is that my story and my words have not only inspired you but have also enlightened you. Never give up on the ones you love and miss.

As I continue to pray for my family, I pray for yours as well. My prayer goes a little something like this:

Dear Heavenly Father,

As we come boldly before Your throne of grace and mercy, we thank You for Your gifts of love, grace, mercy, faith, and forgiveness. We thank You, Lord, for Your ministry of reconciliation.

Lord, we know that You are near and dear to the brokenhearted. We understand Your desire for us to be reconciled one to another. We lift our children unto You, and we lift our grandchildren, our spouses, and our ex-spouses as well. We Pray for Your divine wisdom and guidance within our situations.

We ask that You send them peace and love in a way that they have never experienced before. We ask that You protect them and guide them as You lead them beside the still waters. Please also remind them that we will always love and cherish them. For, no matter how broken the road may be, You have created a pathway that leads us back to one another.

Thank You for giving us the faith, the persever-ance, and the strength we so desperately need to press forward on the behalf of our loved ones. For we know that when the enemy comes rushing in like a flood, Your Spirit, O Lord, will lift up a standard against him. We praise You for that, knowing that all things work together for good to those who love You and are called according to Your purpose.

We pray this in Jesus's Name, as all God's people say, Amen and Hallelujah! We know that what the enemy intended for evil against us, You, O Lord, have and will continue to turn around and use for Your glory!

For Yours is the kingdom, and the power, and the glory, now and forever, Amen!

I wholeheartedly thank each and every one of you for becoming a part of my journey. I look forward to the days ahead, having a hopeful expectation of seeing many families that were once broken being restored and made whole again!

May these words find you and your loved ones well. As my son and I often say, no matter what has happened in the past, "The best is yet to come!"

PLEASE LEAVE A REVIEW

First and foremost, thank you for joining my journey! Now, a request: If you enjoyed reading my memoir, please be kind and leave a review on the site from which you purchased the book. Reviews greatly help both authors and readers, so I look forward to hearing how my story has influenced you.

Also by the Author

My multi-award-winning memoir, *One Man's Journey: The Untold Story of the Quest for Truth*

Scan the QR code to purchase on Amazon:

ABOUT THE AUTHOR

 The author is a man who has sought to live above the norm of what society deems responsible living. He has a passion and a drive to reach the lives and hearts of others. He desires to share his passion with you. While many don't understand it, his mission is to help bring you understanding throughout his book. To contact the author, you may visit his website or email him at the following: https://www.thequestinsearchoftruth.com and thequestinsearchoftruth1@gmail.com.